THE
LITURGICAL
MINISTRY
SERIES

GUIDE FOR SACRISTANS

SECOND EDITION

Corinna Laughlin
Paul Turner

LTP
LITURGY
TRAINING
PUBLICATIONS

Nihil Obstat
Very Reverend Daniel A. Smilanic, JCD
Vicar for Canonical Services
Archdiocese of Chicago
March 29, 2011

Imprimatur
Reverend John F. Canary, STL, DMIN
Vicar General
Archdiocese of Chicago
March 29, 2011

The *Nihil Obstat* and *Imprimatur* are official declarations that a book is free of doctrinal and moral error. No implication is contained therein that those who have granted the *Nihil Obstat* and *Imprimatur* agree with the content, opinions, or statements expressed. Nor do they assume any legal responsibility associated with publication.

Psalm 84:3, 4, 5 and 10, 11

R. How lovely is your dwelling-place, Lord, mighty God!

My soul yearns and pines
*   for the courts of the LORD.*
My heart and my flesh
*   cry out for the living God.*

R. How lovely is your dwelling-place, Lord, mighty God!

Even the sparrow finds a home,
*   and the swallow a nest*
*   in which she puts her young—*
Your altars, O LORD of hosts,
*   my king and my God!*

R. How lovely is your dwelling-place, Lord, mighty God!

Blessed they who dwell in your house!
*   continually they praise you.*
O GOD, behold our shield,
*   and look upon the face of your anointed.*

R. How lovely is your dwelling-place, Lord, mighty God!

I had rather one day in your courts
*   than a thousand elsewhere;*
I had rather lie at the threshold of the house of my God
*   than dwell in the tents of the wicked.*

R. How lovely is your dwelling-place, Lord, mighty God!

Table of Contents

Preface

Go into the village opposite you, and immediately you will find an ass tethered, and a colt with her. Untie them and bring them here to me.

—Matthew 21:2

"He wants us to get *what?*" one disciple asked the other.

"A colt."

"A colt?"

"And an ass."

"*And* an ass? What does the master want with two animals?"

Jesus did not ask his disciples for many things. He usually preached and performed miracles without the assistance of props. Whenever he needed something, his requests were reasonable. At the start of his ministry he received a scroll to read from Isaiah in the synagogue.[1] He used six stone water jars at the wedding in Cana.[2] Twice he asked for a coin—one taken from the mouth of a fish.[3] He got into Simon's boat.[4] He took five loaves and two fish to feed a multitude,[5] and he asked the disciples to gather up the leftover fragments, perhaps to show off a little bit.[6] He asked people to pull the tombstone away from the grave of Lazarus.[7] On the night before he died he wanted a house for Passover.[8] Before leaving the Last Supper he advised the disciples to bring along sacks and swords.[9] He needed a drink on the Cross.[10] After the Resurrection he requested some fresh fish to eat.[11] All in all, he was not very demanding.

So it must have seemed odd that he wanted two rather large animals one Sunday morning outside Jerusalem. Jesus had walked everywhere in his ministry. There is no clear record of him riding a camel, a horse, or a hippo. Out of the blue he said, "Go into the village opposite you, and immediately you will find an ass tethered, and a colt with her. Untie them and bring them here to me."[12]

Did he make some arrangements ahead of time? Did he own these beasts? Did he know that he could borrow them anytime he was in need?

Who was responsible for these animals? How was it that Jesus knew this person?

Jesus continued, "And if anyone should say anything to you, reply, 'The master has need of them.' Then he will send them at once."[13] He never said whether he knew the owner personally, or if he surmised that the owner would be persuaded by this mysterious explanation.

The disciples did as Jesus ordered them. It worked. They unhitched the animals. Then they got into the spirit of it. They took off their cloaks and laid them over the ass and the colt.

Jesus sat on them. He sat on both animals. The other evangelists don't say this, but Matthew is quite explicit. "He sat upon them."[14] It must have been puzzling to see the Son of God straddling two beasts of burden. Yet the sight inspired a very large crowd to remove their cloaks and spread them on the road. The people cut branches from the trees and strewed them on the road, too. The disciples were probably grateful for this help. They didn't have to hack the trees and make all these preparations themselves.

Jesus of Nazareth was making his triumphal entry into the city of Jerusalem. It was the beginning of the end, the first day of the last week of his earthly life. Within days the crowd would turn against him, but on this day he reached the heights of adulation. He was honored as the king whose coming Zechariah foretold: "See, your king shall come to you; / a just savior is he, / Meek, and riding on an ass, / on a colt, the foal of an ass."[15] Matthew reports that Jesus rode two animals in order to make sure no one missed the fulfillment of this prophecy.

The arrival of Jesus required special preparation. He had entered Jerusalem several times before, but he asked for help on this occasion to make the arrangements more magnificent than usual.

Ever since, the Church has relied on special people to help prepare the way of the Lord, people who would appoint a room for Eucharist, prepare the essentials for this holy banquet, straighten things up, and provide for the most unusual requests if they will lend more meaning to the celebration.

Those special people today are called sacristans. They usually work quietly behind closed doors, out of the public eye. But their work is invaluable to the gathered community. When they receive an unusual request, they sometimes wonder, "You want me to get *what*?" But they are ready to fulfill the most unusual requests if it means preparing a path for the entry of our Lord Jesus Christ the King.

Paul Turner

NOTES

1. See Luke 4:17.

2. See John 2:6–7.

3. See Matthew 22:19 and 17:27.

4. See Luke 5:3.

5. See Matthew 14:17–18.

6. See John 6:12.

7. See John 11:39.

8. See Matthew 26:18.

9. See Luke 22:36.

10. See John 19:28.

11. See John 21:10.

12. Matthew 21:2.

13. Matthew 21:3.

14. Matthew 21:7.

15. Zechariah 9:9.

Welcome

You have offered to serve your church as a sacristan. You will be doing the legwork to help other people worship. This book is for you. It aims to help you perform your ministry with understanding, while keeping a spirit of service.

Here you will find information about the storage rooms of churches, the contents of the closets, and the tangible needs of the worshipping community. You will learn what is essential for Mass and how to use items effectively.

You will also learn a little about our history as a Church and what it means for us to gather for Sunday Eucharist and on other occasions. This book will give you spiritual formation as well. It will help you set your heart in the right spirit while serving the needs of the Church.

Sacristans are priceless. If Eucharist is going to be celebrated, somebody has to prepare it. If a meal at home is going to be eaten, somebody has to get it ready. Those who eat rarely show sufficient appreciation to those who did all the work. Yet by the grace of God the work goes on. God knows what you do, and you can be confident of a reward that satisfies beyond human measure.

Second Edition

November 27, 2011, the First Sunday of Advent, was designated as the implementation date for the revised English translation of the Mass texts. Since the original publication of *Guide for Sacristans,* the third edition of *The Roman Missal* received *recognitio* and is being prepared for publication. The implementation of the revised English translation of the Mass texts will take place on November 27, 2011, the First Sunday of Advent. The content in this book has been updated to accurately reflect the new Missal. If you have additional questions regarding *The Roman Missal,* it's history, translation, and pastoral use, please visit LTP's Web site, www.RevisedRomanMissal.org.

About the Authors

This book was written by two authors. Paul Turner wrote the first sections of the book: the preface, "Welcome," "Theology and History of the Sacristan," and "Spirituality and Formation of the Sacristan." He is the pastor of St. Munchin parish in Cameron, Missouri, and its mission, St. Aloysius in Maysville. A priest of the diocese of Kansas City–St. Joseph, he holds a doctorate in sacred theology from Sant' Anselmo in Rome. He is the author of many pastoral resources about sacraments and the liturgy.

Corinna Laughlin wrote the practical description and explanation of the sacristan's duties in the sections titled "Serving as a Sacristan," "Frequently Asked Questions," and has provided the resources section and the glossary. Corinna is the director of liturgy for St. James Cathedral in Seattle. She is also a member of the faculty of the Liturgical Ministries Institute, a training program for lay ministers in the Archdiocese of Seattle. She has written articles for *Pastoral Liturgy*™ and *Today's Liturgy*. Corinna is the author of LTP's *Sourcebook for Sundays, Seasons, and Weekdays: The Almanac for Pastoral Liturgy 2009* and coauthor of *Daily Prayer 2010* with Ward Johnson. She holds a doctorate in English language and literature from the University of Washington and a bachelor's degree in English from Mount Holyoke College. Visit the Web site of St. James Cathedral at www.stjames-cathedral.org.

Questions for Discussion

1. Why have you agreed to serve as a sacristan at your church?

_____

_____

_____

_____

_____

_____

2. What do you hope to gain in your understanding of the theology and function of the ministry through this book?

_____

_____

_____

_____

_____

_____

Theology and History of the Sacristan

---

*How holy this feast in which Christ is our food;
his passion is recalled; grace fills our hearts; and
we receive a pledge of the glory to come.*

—*Saint Thomas Aquinas*

Understanding Your Role

When you set up for Mass, you open up the building and set out the bread, wine, and vessels. The priest and deacon will wear vestments appropriate to the day's liturgy. They and the lectors and readers will pray and proclaim from books marked with ribbons for the day's celebration. Those in the Entrance Procession will hold hymnals, worship aids, or song sheets. You prepare everything in a timely way for the variety of ministers and for the members of the assembly who will worship together at this service.

But what does it all mean? Why do we worry about the color of vestments, the placement of ribbons, the number of hosts, the quantity of wine, or the arrangement of cloths? The simple answer is that it keeps things orderly. But if you step away from the details, you can appreciate the larger purposes for which we gather.

Bread, Wine, and Vessels

Before Mass begins a careful sacristan will set out the correct amount of bread and wine along with the appropriate liturgical vessels. "It is most desirable that the faithful, just as the Priest himself is bound to do; receive the Lord's Body from hosts consecrated at the same Mass and that, in the cases where this is foreseen, they partake of the chalice. . . ."[1]

At first the reason for this action seems obvious. You set out bread and wine because we need them for Holy Communion. But the meaning of this communion concerns our identity as a Church.

Bread and wine have a deep significance. On the surface we use bread and wine because Jesus did. They were common table elements in his day. Today, no matter where Catholics celebrate Mass, they use bread and wine, even in regions where wheat and grapes do not grow. We do not use other local foods indigenous to the regions where we live. We eat and drink what Jesus offered at the Last Supper.

Look more closely at the significance of bread and wine. Grains of wheat must be harvested and milled to become flour. Water is added and the mixture is kneaded and heated for it to become bread. Grapes must be harvested and pressed to become juice. The liquid must be barreled and aged to ferment into wine. One loaf of bread and one bottle of wine may be shared by several people; food and drink make many into one. Thus, bread and wine come to us as a result of adversity, and they bind as one those who consume them. They nurture the body and they refresh the spirit.

This bread and wine become signs and symbols of our sacrifice. They are carried to the altar along with our financial gifts, as a sign that we offer ourselves to God on the altar with Christ. For this reason, the Church encourages the faithful to receive the Lord's Body from hosts consecrated at the same Mass and to partake of the chalice. We offer our gifts; our gifts are transformed; we consume these very same gifts, and we are transformed. Our sacrifice brings an immediate reward. The Holy Spirit takes the "stuff" of our lives and offers it back to us in a new way. When people receive bread and wine consecrated at the very Mass they attend, they participate more deeply in Eucharist.

At Mass the bread and wine become the Body and Blood of Christ. They transform us into a more unified Church. When we gather, we come as the body of Christ to listen to the word of God, to give thanks, to share Holy Communion, and to be sent forth. All this happens because Christ is truly present in our midst.

When we share Holy Communion, we become one with Christ and with one another. We form ourselves as a local church, but we also express our solidarity with the universal Church. Pope John Paul II expressed it this way: "each community, gathering all its members for the 'breaking of the bread,' becomes the place where the mystery of the Church is concretely made present. In celebrating the Eucharist, the community opens itself to communion with the universal Church."[2]

When sacristans set out bread and wine along with the vessels for Eucharist, they prepare us all to express our thanks, to offer our sacrifice, to affirm our unity, and to be sent into the world as the body of Christ.

Vestments, Books, and the Liturgical Year

Priests, deacons, and servers wear special vestments at Mass. The *Lectionary for Mass* and *The Roman Missal* (formerly called *The Sacramentary*) need to be marked with the readings and prayers of the day. Some ministers perform these duties themselves. Others rely on the sacristan to help.

This duty is more than stagecraft. It isn't a matter of choosing costumes and marking pages so that the ceremony looks and sounds right. When you sort through the vestments and books of the liturgy, you enter the flow of the liturgical year.

The Catholic Church observes a detailed calendar of liturgical time, and a good sacristan will be familiar with them.

Sunday anchors the liturgical year. It is the Lord's Day. It commemorates the Resurrection. Every Sunday is a little celebration of Easter.

Other liturgical days are grouped in order of their significance. Solemnities are the principal days in the calendar, such as Easter, Nativity of the Lord, Epiphany of the Lord, Ascension of the Lord, and Pentecost. They also include the days honoring the Nativity of Saint John the Baptist (June 24), the martyrdoms of Saint Peter and Saint Paul (June 29), and the Immaculate Conception of the Blessed Virgin Mary (December 8). The principal patrons of the local church, as well as its anniversary of dedication, are all celebrated as solemnities.

Feasts take the next rank. These honor some events in the life of Christ, such as the Presentation of the Lord (February 2) and the

> ✠ "Holy Church celebrates the saving work of Christ on prescribed days in the course of the year with sacred remembrance. Each week, on the day called the Lord's Day, she commemorates the Resurrection of the Lord, which she also celebrates once a year in the great Paschal Solemnity, together with his blessed Passion. In fact, throughout the course of the year the Church unfolds the entire mystery of Christ and observes the birthdays of the Saints."
>
> —*Universal Norms on the Liturgical Year and the General Roman Calendar, 1*

Transfiguration of the Lord (August 6). Others remember Mary, the apostles, or the archangels, such as the feasts of Our Lady of Guadalupe (December 12); Saint Matthew (September 21); and Saint Michael, Saint Gabriel, and Saint Raphael (September 29).

Memorials call to mind other saints of universal influence, such as Saint Mary Magdalene (July 22), Saint Thomas Aquinas (January 28), and Saint Augustine (August 28). Optional memorials appear on the universal calendar, but local churches may choose whether or not to observe them. They make this choice depending on their devotion to the saint in question, for example, Saint Romuald (June 19), Saint Elizabeth of Portugal (July 4), and Saint Louis (August 25).

All other days are simply referred to as "weekdays," no matter when they fall.

The liturgical year begins with Advent, which starts on the fourth Sunday before Nativity of the Lord and prepares us to celebrate the first coming as we anticipate the second coming of Christ. Christmas Time celebrates the birth of Jesus. Lent begins on the Wednesday preceding the sixth Sunday before Easter. The Paschal Triduum consists of the three days leading up to Easter Time, celebrating the Passion, Death, and Resurrection of Christ. Easter Day falls on the Sunday following the first full moon of spring. Easter Time extends for 50 days and concludes with Pentecost, when we celebrate the coming of the Holy Spirit into the Church.

The rest of the calendar is called "Ordinary Time." It begins when Christmas Time concludes.[3] It is interrupted by Lent and Easter Time, resuming after Pentecost and continuing until the end of the liturgical year. The last Sunday of the year is the solemnity of Our Lord Jesus Christ, King of the Universe. After the following weekdays have run their course, the new liturgical year begins again with the First Sunday of Advent.

When we honor the liturgical year, we proclaim Christ as the Lord of all time and all ages. Sunday is the anchor of all liturgical time. Already in the New Testament, the Lord's Day[4] was becoming the significant day for prayer. It was the day on which Jesus rose from the dead,[5] the day on which he appeared to some followers,[6] a day for the early Church to break bread[7] and collect contributions for the needy.[8]

When we gather on Sundays we proclaim our faith in the Resurrection, our love for the community, our openness to the word, and

> *Do not be afraid to give your time to Christ!*
>
> —*Pope John Paul II*

our acceptance of our common mission. Sunday is for worship and for rest. In a culture that promotes constant activity and stimulation, rest is all the more valuable.

There is no better way to honor Sunday than to give some of our time to Christ. Pope John Paul II wrote, "*Do not be afraid to give your time to Christ!* Yes, let us open our time to Christ, that he may cast light upon it and give it direction. He is the One who knows the secret of time and the secret of eternity, and he gives us 'his day' as an ever new gift of his love."[9]

When sacristans set out vestments and books, they help the assembled faithful participate in the mystery of sacred time. People already know that this hour at church will have a special quality, that it will be more sacred than other moments of the week. They know that their own time is precious, and they protect it as the treasure that it is. As they gather for worship, they come at a special time for a length of time into a certain kind of time that is only a part of all time. The colors, readings, and prayers of the Mass all contribute to the specific nature of the sacred time at hand.[10]

What's more, this time together now is preparing the Church for its time together in eternity. Jesus said, "Whoever eats my flesh and drinks my blood has eternal life."[11] Our Eucharist is a foretaste of the heavenly banquet that Christ has prepared for us. When we step into church at the time for Mass, we remove ourselves from ordinary life, and we enter a space and time that belong elsewhere—that belong in a place where we all belong, and for which we most long to be.

Saint Thomas Aquinas wrote a beautiful verse about Eucharist, known by its Latin title *O sacrum convivium*. It expresses the future hope of the eucharistic meal: "How holy this feast in which Christ is our food; his passion is recalled; grace fills our hearts; and we receive a pledge of the glory to come."[12]

The Church

All the activity with vessels, vestments, books, bread and wine takes place inside a building we call a church because the people who gather there are the Church. Sacristans know their way around the building—and also around the people.

The primary ministers perform their actions in the sanctuary, while the faithful worship from the nave. Many churches have a narthex or gathering area—indoors or outdoors. Churches may have choir lofts and basements, brides' rooms and ushers' rooms, places for child care as well as for catechumens, baptistries, and reconciliation rooms.

The area the sacristan probably knows the best is the sacristy, a kind of staging area adjacent to the main spaces. Many churches have both a working sacristy and a vesting sacristy. The first holds the liturgical vessels and is usually located near the sanctuary. The vesting sacristy holds the vestments and may be located near the front door from where ministers will process to the altar through the assembled faithful.

Additionally there may be storage areas, closets, and drawers of various sizes. Catholic churches accumulate quite an array of articles used in worship. Many of them are passed on from one generation to another. Sacristans will be familiar with all these storage areas and their contents. They will probably need to clean house every once in a while.

> *The sacristan's affection for the inanimate is only a sign of affection for the people who are the Church.*

The sacristan's affection for the inanimate building is only a sign of affection for the people who are the Church. The building is the place where we express our common faith. It holds the memories of weddings, Baptisms, confessions, and funerals. It is alive with tradition and innovation, insight, and mercy.

Throughout the building the sacristan takes care of the candles for the Easter Vigil, ashes for the beginning of Lent, charcoal for incense, the pall that covers the coffin at funerals, and the chrism that anoints the newly baptized. Nearly every ritual in the year employs something physical that opens up the spiritual world.

Catholic piety is rooted in the "stuff" of the earth: bread, wine, oil, palms, and ashes. We set a table, a chair, and a reading desk in the sanctuary. We decorate the church with statues and images of people who became saints. All of these things lead us to God, whose Son took on the stuff of the earth, becoming human at the Incarnation.

The church building is another sign of the sacredness of the people who worship there and the God who lives there. The sacristan cares for this space with the reverence due to the house of God and the people who praise, repent, adore, and petition within its walls.

History of Your Role

The word "sacristy" means a place for sacred things. By the fifth century, ministers of the liturgy started designating a room for vessels and vestments, cloths and candles, books, and other appurtenances. It only made sense to store these items where they could be found and retrieved, and where they could be secured following the service.

The same place was also used for the vesting of ministers. Before the service began, ministers needed a place to don liturgical garb. As sacristies were the rooms where the garb was kept, ministers started dressing there, where they pulled the vestments from a closet.

The earliest sacristies were located near the sanctuary. Again, practicality ruled the decision. In the past, vested ministers usually made a direct entrance from the sacristy to the sanctuary. If a more elaborate procession was desired, ministers could vest elsewhere or unceremoniously move from the sacristy to the front of the church where they could begin a grander entrance.

The size of the sacristy depended on its usage. In some smaller churches, a compartment near the altar sufficed for storage. But in larger places, especially cathedrals and historic churches where many clergy might vest at a time, the sacristy became quite large, even encompassing a suite of rooms. In many churches, for example, priests and servers vested in separate sacristies.

The main sacristy was often pierced with doors giving access to the sanctuary, the nave, and to the outside of the church. The ministers arriving for the service could walk from outside directly into the sacristy, and from the sacristy to the sanctuary, without making much contact with the people in the nave. For many centuries, the priest celebrated the Mass in a low voice while the people offered different though simultaneous prayer. Sacristies were designed to facilitate this separation.

After the Council of Trent, sacristies became more elaborate. The Council recommended that the sacristan be a priest or a cleric, but this would eventually prove impractical. The size and decoration of sacristies grew with a stunning artistic development. Many sacristies from this period are works of art from floor to ceiling and from wall to closet. One of the most famous is the new sacristy for St. Lawrence Church in Florence, Italy, designed by Michelangelo and embellished with his statues for the tombs of the Medicis.

Sacristies were being used for a variety of purposes. They became museums for works of art, places where relics and treasures were kept. The ambry for the reposition of holy oils was often retained in the sacristy, as was the sacrarium, the special sink with a pipe leading directly into the earth; it was used during the cleansing of Communion vessels for an honorable discarding of the rinse. Candles, cloths, vessels, and incense were all stored in the sacristies. And some of them had tombs.

The role of the sacristan grew over a period of time. The position was filled by a respected person in the community who would handle donations for Mass stipends and keep the parish records orderly. For a while the person known as the porter opened and closed the church, rang the bell, and fulfilled a host of other responsibilities from cleaning the floor to digging graves. In the Middle Ages, the Roman Church asked men preparing for the priesthood to be formally admitted into the preliminary order of porter during a ceremony over which a Bishop presided. The role became more ceremonial than functional, and the practical duties were turned over to qualified laypeople.

In some churches the sacristy is called the vestry, referring to its function as the place where ministers dress. In other churches the responsible person has been called the sexton, a title that derived from the word *sacristan*.

Today a sacristy can be a lively room where several ministers gather before and after the service. But the *General Instruction of the Roman Missal* (GIRM) has requested that silence be observed in the sacristy as much as possible before Mass begins.[13] For the sake of maintaining order and a proper spirit for worship, it helps if someone is designated as the sacristan.

Questions for Discussion and Reflection

1. How did you first become interested in becoming a sacristan?

_____

_____

_____

2. Who inspired you in this ministry?

_____

_____

_____

3. Why is the sacristan's role important? Is it purely functional—getting things ready for Mass? Or is there a spiritual side to it? What makes the preparation of the church a spiritual exercise?

_____

_____

_____

NOTES

1. *General Instruction of the Roman Missal* (GIRM), 85.

2. *Dies Domini,* 34.

3. Christmas Time ends with the feast of the Baptism of the Lord.

4. See Revelation 1:10.

5. See Mark 16:2 and 9; Luke 24:1; John 20:1.

6. See Luke 24:13–36; John 20:19.

7. See Acts 20:7–12.

8. See 1 Corinthians 16:2.

9. *Dies Domini,* 7.

10. Please see page 30 for more information regarding the practicalities of preparing ritual books for Mass and other special rites.

11. John 6:54.

12. Canticle of Mary, Evening Prayer II, Solemnity of the Most Holy Body and Blood of Christ (*Corpus Christi*), Liturgy of the Hours, volume 3.

13. See GIRM, 45.

Spirituality and Formation of the Sacristan

How lovely is your dwelling place, Lord, mighty God! I had rather one day in your courts than a thousand elsewhere.

—Psalm 84:3, 10

Reflections on Your Ministry

A sacristan usually works behind the scenes and outside the actual celebration of the liturgy. The sacristan's role is very different from that of the reader and extraordinary minister of Holy Communion, for example, who serve in front of others, in positions where they are the focus of attention while the liturgy is going on. The sacristan is different, and many sacristans like it that way.

Jesus said, when you help others, "Do not blow a trumpet before you, as the hypocrites do in the synagogues and in the streets to win the praise of others."[1] Instead, "Do not let your left hand know what your right hand is doing. . . . Your Father who sees in secret will repay you."[2] The sacristan often works in secret and enjoys the status of an essential, though anonymous helper.

I'm opening up the church, Lord.
I hold the keys that break the seal between the night outside
*   and your light within.*
Soon people will pass through the doors that I unlock.
Help them leave behind their concerns.
Help them enter into your presence.
And help me serve you and them on both sides of these doors.
Amen.

Your basic work as a sacristan is to help with Mass, but other celebrations will also need your aid. As you reflect on your role, let the liturgy of the Church form you into an ever better minister.

You have been building your spirituality throughout your life. You have found consolation in participating at Mass, reading from the Bible, sitting down with a favorite prayer book, saying the Rosary, or offering some other devotions. As a sacristan you may deepen your spiritual life by a reflection on the Church's liturgy that you help prepare.

Somewhere on a sacristy shelf you will find the liturgical books necessary for celebrating the various rites of the Catholic Church. The spiritual exercises on the next pages are intended to help you become more familiar with these books and to recommit to the specific service that you give.

Each one of these books contains a treasury of rituals, prayers, and instructions. This section will not treat all the books and all their contents, but it will give you a taste for the wealth of ritual that has evolved in the Catholic Church.

Rite of Christian Initiation of Adults and Rite of Baptism for Children

The single book called the *Rite of Christian Initiation of Adults* is a collection of many rites primarily for moving unbaptized adults through the stages of a catechumenate, up to their initiation, and beyond. The book also includes the Rite of Reception of Baptized Christians into the Full Communion of the Catholic Church. Some people wishing to join the Catholic Church have already been baptized; this rite of reception is for them.

The same book also treats other circumstances: the Confirmation and first Holy Communion of adult Catholics who were baptized but never received formal catechesis afterward; the Christian initiation of unbaptized children of catechetical age (about the age of six and older); and Christian initiation in unusual circumstances, such as the danger of death.

If those to be baptized are children younger than catechetical age, the minister conducts this ceremony using the book called the *Rite of Baptism for Children*. Many of the elements from the rites of adult initiation are included in this book as well.

Look over the table of contents in these books and see the many ritual opportunities they present. Almost all of these rites need the help of a sacristan—at least to set out the right book!

As a sacristan, you could be asked to prepare any number of items and make special arrangements. Think about what your actions are preparing for and how you might set your heart as you help people celebrate the various stages of initiation.

Seating. You may need to reserve some seats for catechumens, candidates, parents, godparents, and sponsors. As you do so, think about these people. Do you know their names? Do you know what has moved them to join the Catholic Church, to present a child for Baptism, or to sponsor someone making this spiritual journey? What is your relationship to these people? They will soon be sharing Holy Communion with you at the table of the Lord. How are you the body of Christ for them?

Think about what these reserved seats mean to these people. Catechumens have wanted to belong to this Church community, and now they have a reserved seat. They are being treated as special guests, but one day they will be like others, just a part of the family.

In your home, when do you arrange seating? Where do you want everyone to sit when you gather for a meal, when you have a meeting, or when you are passing the time? Are there some chairs used only by someone special? How do you want guests to feel when they enter and take their place in your home?

Jesus said, "I confer a kingdom on you, just as my Father has conferred one on me, that you may eat and drink at my table in my kingdom."
—*Luke 22:29–30*

As you set out the reserved signs, what is your prayer for the people who will occupy those seats? What is your prayer for yourself? Who are you for them? Who do you want to be for them?

Processional cross. In the Rite of Acceptance into the Order of Catechumens, some parishes use a processional cross for the first acceptance of the Gospel.[3]

During this celebration, those who are unbaptized petition the Church for the gifts of faith and eternal life. In response we accept them into the community of those preparing for Baptism, a community called the order of catechumens.

During this dialogue between the inquirers and the priest or deacon, a server may stand nearby, holding the processional cross as a visual symbol of the life, suffering and promise that Christ offers his disciples.

Jesus said, "Just as Moses lifted up the serpent in the desert, so must the Son of Man be lifted up, so that everyone who believes in him may have eternal life."

—*John 3:14–15*

Look at the processional cross in your church. What does it say to you? What cross do you carry in your life? Is it a cross of pain or a cross of hope? When you see a minister carry the cross in procession, lifted high and put in motion and the head of the people, what does that proclaim about our faith?

When you set the processional cross out for the Rite of Acceptance, what is your prayer for those who will become catechumens? How do you want Jesus to touch them? What virtue will they need to follow Christ? How will your parish community be Christ for them? How will your personal story of faith bear witness to the power of the Cross of Christ?

Crosses. The same rite allows someone to present a cross to each of those being accepted into the order of catechumens.[4] Some other symbolic act could take place, or this gesture may be omitted. But in some parishes, the catechumens receive a cross they may pin on their lapel, carry in their pocket, or hang on a wall at home.

Jesus said to all, "If anyone wishes to come after me, he must deny himself and take up his cross daily and follow me."

—*Luke 9:23*

Where are the crosses that you own? Do you have several of them at home? Where did they come from? What does it mean to have them hang where they do? Do you have a cross in your possession right now—a decorative item or a religious medal or part of a Rosary? On what occasions do you have a cross on your person? Why?

As you set out the crosses for the catechumens, what is your prayer for them? What do you want them to accomplish with this cross? What do you want this cross to accomplish for them?

Bibles. The same rite allows someone to present a book containing the Gospel to those who are becoming catechumens.[5] That book may be the *Lectionary for Mass*, the *Book of the Gospels*, or a Bible that catechumens may take home with them. Some parishes have them reverence the book commonly used at church for the proclamation of the scriptures; others give the catechumens their own book. The Bible will become a kind of textbook for them. The word of God more than any other source will form them as followers of Christ.

How do you use your Bible? Do you turn to it frequently for prayer? Which passages are your favorites? What does the Bible mean for you? Where do you keep your Bible at home? Why there?

Are the Lectionary and Book of the Gospels stored in a special place at your church? Or are they put on a shelf with more common books because they happen to fit there? When you set them out, do you handle

> *The word of God is living and effective, sharper than any two-edged sword, penetrating even between soul and spirit, joints and marrow, and able to discern reflections and thoughts of the heart.*
>
> —*Hebrews 4:12*

them with reverence? When you participate at Mass, are you attentive to the word of God as it is proclaimed in the community? How do you listen for the voice of Jesus in the Gospel?

As you set out the Lectionary, *Book of the Gospels*, or the Bibles for the catechumens, what are you thinking about? How would you like them to use the scripture in their life? Are you a good model for them? Would they benefit hearing from you about your love for the scriptures?

The oil of catechumens. During the period of the catechumenate, adults may be anointed with the oil of catechumens one or more times.[6] It may happen at a special gathering of the catechumens with their sponsors and other members of the community, or it could even take place at a Sunday Mass.

When infants are baptized, the priest or deacon may anoint them with the oil of catechumens early in the service.[7] This anointing is optional, but many ministers use this oil as a pre-baptismal anointing.

In some places, adults are anointed with the oil of catechumens during the Easter Vigil after they renounce sin and before they profess their faith in Christ.

This oil is blessed by the Bishop at the Chrism Mass each year shortly before the end of Lent. If your parish runs out, your priest or deacon may bless more. This is a pre-baptismal oil. It is administered only to those who are not yet baptized. They may be anointed beneath the throat or on the palms of their hands.

This is an oil of protection. It is used in conjunction with prayers for freedom from sin and the powers of temptation. Once the prayer has expelled evil, the oil of catechumens is applied to keep it out. It works

Jesus unrolled the scroll and found the passage where it was written: "The Spirit of the Lord is upon me, / because he has anointed me / to bring glad tidings to the poor. / He has sent me to proclaim liberty to captives / and recovery of sight to the blind, / to let the oppressed go free, / and to proclaim a year acceptable to the Lord."

—*Luke 4:17–19*

like sunscreen. It wards off perilous powers that can harm a person unprotected by Baptism; in this case, it guards against the power of evil and the temptation to sin.

How do you protect yourself from evil? Do you rely on prayer, the company of other Christians, or the practice of good works? What have you found effective? How did you learn that? From where do you draw your spiritual strength to avoid sinful habits?

What types of protective oils do you use at home? Mosquito repellent? Topical medicines? What are your hopes for them? When you put them on, you admit you are weak without some additional help.

As you set out the oil of catechumens, what is your prayer for those who are still unbaptized? How do you want God to protect them? What in our society and culture might infect them without the support of the people of God? Whether the unbaptized person is an infant or an adult, what are you asking God to do?

Book of the Elect. The Rite of Election usually takes place on or near the First Sunday of Lent at the cathedral church of the diocese. The Bishop usually presides. During the ceremony he announces that the catechumens are "elect" or named among the chosen people of the new covenant of Baptism. The highlight of this rite is the signing of the book and the proclamation of the Bishop.[8] But in some dioceses, the book—or a loose page to be inserted later into the book—is signed in parishes. That takes place during a ceremony called the Rite of Sending of the Catechumens for Election.[9] If this takes place in your parish, you may need to set out a page or the *Book of the Elect*.

When catechumens sign the *Book of the Elect*, they indicate their firm desire to celebrate the rites of initiation, and the Bishop declares that they will indeed celebrate Baptism, Confirmation, and Eucharist at the Easter Vigil in just a few weeks. The book is a sign of God's call, and the signature is a sign of one's commitment.

When do you sign your name? Think over the past week or so. When did you do it? Did you sign letters? Checks? Did you initial a contract? Sign a receipt for your credit card? In the world of electronic communication, your identification is automatically made known when you e-mail someone, send a text message, or make a phone call. But when do you actually pick up a pen and write your name? It's usually for something special. How does it feel? Does it feel more personal when you write your name out?

> *If you confess with your mouth that Jesus is Lord and believe in your heart that God raised him from the dead, you will be saved.*
>
> —*Romans 10:9*

Do it now, just for the experience. Take a piece of paper and a pen and write your name. How does that feel? What does your signature symbolize?

As you prepare the church for the Rite of Sending, what are your prayers for the catechumens? They are going to put their name on the line. Would you be willing to do the same thing for your faith? How will they inspire you? How will you inspire them? This coming week, what do you need to be committed to? To what will you sign your name?

Font. Churches have baptismal fonts, but you may need to prepare the water— and in some cases, to prepare the font.

Fonts have changed in shapes and appearance. For many centuries they almost all resembled a bowl resting on a pillar. The font was large enough to catch the water poured from a shell over the head of an infant. These fonts were often located in small chapels, sized to fit the few people who attended an infant's Baptism.

Today Baptism by immersion has

> *Are you unaware that we who were baptized into Christ Jesus were baptized into his death? We were indeed buried with him through baptism into death, so that, just as Christ was raised from the dead by the glory of the Father, we too might live in newness of life.*
>
> —*Romans 6:3–4*

become more popular in many places, and fonts are bigger. For infant Baptism the bowl is large enough for the priest or deacon to lower the child into the water[10] and for adult Baptism the font is large enough to accommodate one or more adults.[11] The sacristan will have to prepare a large quantity of water in either case.

It is permissible to baptize with a temporary font set up in the sanctuary.[12] This will allow a larger congregation to witness the proceedings. A sacristan may need to set it up prior to the celebration.

You use water at home in many ways. You drink it for life. You bathe in it for cleanliness. You wash with it, brush with it, and flush with it. You keep goldfish in it. Water gives life; it can also take it away.

As you prepare water for those to be baptized, think of all its properties. It is going to bestow new life in Christ. It will forgive sin. It will destroy the power of evil. What is your prayer for the children and adults who will be baptized? What are you asking Christ for them? How do you hope they will be changed? What has your Baptism meant to you? How does it influence your life each day? Think on this the next time you renew your baptismal promises or sign yourself with holy water.

The one who gives us security with you in Christ and who anointed us is God; he has also put his seal upon us and given the Spirit in our hearts as a first installment.

—*2 Corinthians 1:21*

Sacred Chrism. Chrism is a perfumed oil that can be consecrated only by a bishop. It is used solemnly in Baptism, Confirmation, Holy Orders, and the dedication of a church or altar. You may have to set out the chrism for the celebration of Baptism[13] or Confirmation in your parish.[14]

The Holy Spirit is especially powerful through the use of chrism. We use this oil for events that happen once in a lifetime. Its power never ends.

When do you use perfumes? Every day? Do you have some you use only for special occasions? Why?

Put on then, as God's chosen ones, holy and beloved, heartfelt compassion, kindness, humility, gentleness, and patience, bearing with one another and forgiving one another, if one has a grievance against another; as the Lord has forgiven you, so must you also do. And over all these put on love, that is, the bond of perfection.

—*Colossians 3:12–14*

Do you remember your Baptism or Confirmation? Do you remember being anointed with chrism?

Find the chrism in your church. It may be kept in an ambry or other special case. Open it up and smell its aroma. Does it remind you of anything in particular? What memories does it evoke?

As you set out chrism for Baptism or Confirmation, think about those who will soon be anointed, and think about the Holy Spirit. How has the Holy Spirit helped you in your life? What is your prayer for those to be anointed? How would you like the Holy Spirit to form them?

White garments. After the newly baptized have been anointed with chrism, they are given white garments.[15] In some parishes these are purely ceremonial—a cloth that lies on top of other clothing. But in others the newly baptized don an entirely new white garment. It symbolizes their new life in Christ, their membership within the body of Christ, and their citizenship in heaven, whose dwellers are frequently depicted in the New Testament clad in white.[16]

When was the last time you bought new clothes? Was it for a special occasion? How did the clothes make you feel? What clothing do you wear when you want to feel as though you belong to a group? Do you ever wear a uniform? Which one and why? What clothing do you wear to church?

As you prepare the white garments for those to be baptized, what is your prayer for them? How has Baptism clothed you with Christ? How do you put on Christ every morning? How will you be Christ for these new Christians?

Paschal and baptismal candles. A new Paschal candle is prepared for the Vigil each year, and it burns every day throughout Easter Time. We also light this candle for Baptisms[17] and funerals,[18] as a reminder of our participation in the Resurrection of Christ. You will set the candle out and light it whenever Baptisms are celebrated.

> *For you were once darkness, but now you are light in the Lord. Live as children of light, for light produces every kind of goodness and righteousness and truth.*
>
> —*Ephesians 5:8–9*

The Paschal candle is a symbol of Christ, whose rising shatters the darkness of sin and death. Lighting a baptismal candle from the Paschal candle shows that one has been enlightened by Christ and will keep the flame of faith alive, until Jesus comes again, as did the wise virgins in the parable,[19] those who awaited the coming of the bridegroom.

When do you use candles at home? Do you use them on the table for meals? In the bedroom for ambience? In a prayer room for inspiration?

Light a candle. Watch its flame glow brightly. Watch the wax yield to the fire. A candle spends itself in order to give its light.

As you prepare candles for Baptism, what is your prayer for those to be baptized? How do you want Christ to light their way? What will they have to yield to follow him? What have you yielded in order to follow Christ your light?

Bread and wine. The most important elements you set out for the initiation rites are the most common elements you prepare for any Mass: bread and wine. Whenever adults are baptized and confirmed, their initiation reaches its climax with Eucharist.[20]

As they eat this bread and drink this cup, they will proclaim the death of the Lord until he comes again. They will share the sacred meal, experiencing unity with the rest of the community, and receiving a foretaste of the life to come.

For I received from the Lord what I also handed on to you, that the Lord Jesus, on the night he was handed over, took bread, and, after he had given thanks, broke it and said, "This is my body that is for you. Do this in remembrance of me." In the same way also the cup, after supper, saying, "This cup is the new covenant in my blood. Do this, as often as you drink it, in remembrance of me." For as often as you eat this bread and drink the cup, you proclaim the death of the Lord until he comes.

—1 Corinthians 11:23–26

At home, when do you eat bread? Do you ever bake your own? Do you know the experience of working the dough at watching it rise, baking it and smelling the aroma that no other bouquet can match? What does bread tell you about creation and the Creator?

With whom do you break bread? Who are your usual tablemates? How would you describe your community? What binds you together? What challenges do you face? How does the meal help? Do expectations come with your meal?

Is someone supposed to perform some service when the meal has ended?

Do you provide wine with meals? On what occasions? Why? What does wine symbolize for you? What did it mean for Jesus?

As you set out the bread and the wine to be shared in Holy Communion for the newly baptized, what is your prayer for them? How do you want them to be broken and outpoured? How will you feel when they eat and drink with you? What will you do to help them experience a foretaste of the heavenly banquet?

The Rite of Penance

The sacristan probably has few responsibilities when it comes to weekly confessions. Usually the confessional or reconciliation room is prepared and ready. But if a communal penance service is to take place during Advent or Lent, for example, a sacristan may be needed to set up stations for reconciliation.[21]

As people approach these stations, they will confess their sins to a priest. He will say the words of absolution, and through the power of the Holy Spirit, sinners are forgiven.

When you prepare the church building for the Rite of Penance, you are preparing church people for one of the most extraordinary experiences in Catholicism: the forgiveness of sins.

And all this is from God, who has reconciled us to himself through Christ and given us the ministry of reconciliation, namely, God was reconciling the world to himself in Christ, not counting their trespasses against them and entrusting to us the message of reconciliation.

—2 Corinthians 5:18–19

When did you last experience forgiveness? Did you confess your guilt to someone else, or did someone say "I'm sorry" to you? Did you achieve reconciliation? Or do you still have pangs of painful regret?

As you prepare the reconciliation stations, what is your prayer for those who will confess their sins? What words do you want the priests to have? How will you be an ambassador of reconciliation in Christ?

Pastoral Care of the Sick

When a member of the community is seriously ill, the priest may offer the Sacrament of Anointing of the Sick as a sign of the Church's pastoral care.

People who come to be anointed are those facing surgery or in a perilous condition of health brought on by age or other factors. As a sacristan, you may need to set out the oil of the sick for this celebration.

The Bishop of the diocese blesses the oil of the sick at the Chrism Mass each year near the end of Lent. If the parish runs out, your priest may bless more.

During the rite, the priest will impose his hands on the sick and anoint their hands with oil.[22]

How do you take care of yourself when you are sick? Who are the healers you turn to? Are they all in the field of medicine, or are they other trusted professionals or friends?

Is anyone among you sick? He should summon the presbyters of the church, and they should pray over him and anoint [him] with oil in the name of the Lord, and the prayer of faith will save the sick person, and the Lord will raise him up. If he has committed any sins, he will be forgiven.

—James 5:14–15

When do you use oil for healing at home? What ailments does oil soothe? How does it feel to have oil rubbed on you?

As you set out the oil for the sick, what is your prayer for them? What ailments do you suffer as you come to this celebration? What powers of healing do you bring?

Celebration and Rest

Sunday is a day for celebration and rest. You gather with your brothers and sisters to celebrate Eucharist, and you enjoy some time for rest. As a sacristan who will have work to do on Sunday, do not forget to perform both these activities.

After you have set up for Mass, celebrate Mass with your brothers and sisters in Christ. Find a good seat in the assembly, join in the singing, make the responses, and share the peace. Enter the Communion Procession and rejoice in the gift of the Body and Blood of Christ.

Sunday is also a day for rest. Refrain from your normal activities. Do something that relaxes you. Spend time with family and friends. Pursue one of your hobbies. Play with children. You will be refreshed to return to your labors.

Sunday rest is a foretaste of heaven. Just as the Sunday Eucharist prepares us for the banquet of eternal life, so Sunday rest prepares us for the peacefulness that awaits us on the last day. If you rest well, you experience a little bit of heaven.

Work hard. God expects you to do that, and your community needs it. But rest well, too. God also expects that, and your community needs you to be a whole person, one who breathes in rest and breathes out work. When you have prepared yourself as a child of God, you do the work of a sacristan: you make ready the holy temple where the Spirit of God has chosen to abide.

NOTES

1. Matthew 6:2.

2. Matthew 6:3–4.

3. See RCIA, 52.

4. See RCIA, 59.

5. See RCIA, 64.

6. See RCIA, 98 - 103.

7. See the *Rite of Baptism for Children* (RBC), 49–51.

8. See RCIA, 132 - 133.

9. See RCIA, 113.

10. See RBC, 60.

11. See RCIA, 226.

12. See RCIA, 218.

13. See RBC, 62.

14. See RCIA, 231–235.

15. See RCIA, 229; RBC, 63.

16. See, for example, Matthew 17:2; 28:3; Mark 16:5; John 20:12; Acts 1:10; Revelation 1:14; 2:17; 3:4; 3:18; 4:4; 6:11; 7:9; 7:13; 15:6.

17. See RCIA, 230; RBC, 64.

18. See the *Order of Christian Funerals* (OCF), 35.

19. See Matthew 25:7.

20. See RCIA, 243.

21. See the *Rite of Penance* (RP), 55.

22. See the *Pastoral Care of the Sick* (PCS), 141.

Serving as a Sacristan

For these sacristans, that the preparations they make for the celebration of the liturgy may remind us to prepare our hearts for worship . . . .

—*Book of Blessings, #1853*

Role of the Sacristan

The sacristan prepares the "things that are necessary"[1] for the celebration of the liturgy: the books, the vestments, the vessels, the bread, and the wine. But the sacristan does more than prepare the *things* needed for worship: the sacristan's reverent, prayerful preparation can remind the entire assembly to prepare their *hearts* for worship.[2]

As you have seen in the first section of this book, much of the sacristan's time is spent "behind the scenes," so to speak. Most often, the sacristan's work is done before the liturgy begins. But this quiet, even invisible ministry is very important. After all, if the church doors are not open, the assembly cannot gather. If the books are not ready, the word cannot be proclaimed. If the bread and wine are not prepared, the Mass cannot be celebrated. The work of the sacristan really matters.

✠ "The sacristan, . . . diligently arranges the liturgical books, the vestments and other things that are necessary in the celebration of Mass."

—GIRM, 105a

A Walk through the Sacristy

Sacristies come in all shapes and sizes, ranging from tiny closets with just enough room to turn around in to chapel-sized spaces with roomy cupboards, wide vesting tables, and stained-glass windows. All sacristies serve the same function, however: to house the holy things that will be necessary for worship, and to provide a space for ministers to prepare for the celebration.

Vessels

Vessels are usually kept in a vault or designated cupboard. These include chalices, along with the cups used for the entire assembly when Holy Communion is given under both kinds. Other vessels include pitchers or carafes in which the wine is brought forward at the Presentation and Preparation of the Gifts and subsequently transferred into chalices, cruets for the mingling of the water with the wine, and pitchers and basins for the priest's washing of hands during the Mass. There are also patens, ciboria, or bowls for the hosts. Monstrances—special receptacles in which a consecrated host is displayed for veneration—and sometimes reliquaries containing the relic of a saint can be found in the sacristy.

The Roman Missal, *chalice, and paten placed on the corporal for the celebration of the Eucharist.*

Vestments

Vestments for the clergy and for lay ministers are also kept in the sacristy. The most important of these are the chasubles, the priestly vestment which is worn only for the celebration of Mass. It is usually an ample garment, which is placed over the head and falls in loose folds almost to the feet. A full set of chasubles include white, green, violet, and red. Additional colors may also be used—rose, black, gold, and silver. Each chasuble usually has a distinctive stole that matches it in color and texture.

In addition to chasubles, the sacristy will likely also hold vestments for the deacon: dalmatics in the liturgical colors, and diaconal stoles, which are draped over the left shoulder, drawn diagonally across the chest, and pinned at the right side. The dalmatic is a tunic in shape. Like the chasuble, it is an outer garment worn in the liturgical colors.

Among the other vestments in the sacristy one might also find a cope (a mantle or cape, which clasps at the neck). The cope is worn for liturgies outside of the Mass—for example, for the Liturgy of the Hours—and for certain processions, like the procession of palms on Palm Sunday. Copes, too, are made in the liturgical colors, and they can be worn by a Bishop, priest, or deacon. The cope is generally worn with alb and stole.

A sacristan helps a lay liturgical minister vest in an alb.

Albs, cassocks, and surplices may also be stored in the sacristy. The alb is the most ancient liturgical vestment—a long, white tunic reaching to the feet. The alb is a baptismal garment, which is why any of the baptized may wear it. It may be worn by all the ministers of the liturgy, both clergy and lay. The surplice is the short white garment worn over a cassock. A cassock may be black or some other color. It may be worn by both clergy and lay ministers (such as acolytes, servers, choir members) in liturgical rites. Some clergy wear it as "house" dress.

You may also find humeral veils, used for Solemn Exposition and Benediction of the Holy Eucharist and for eucharistic processions, as on Holy Thursday. This long, rectangular piece of ornamental fabric is fitted with clasps, so that (with the help of another minister) the priest or deacon can attach it around his neck, and then place the ends of the veil around the monstrance or ciborium. A vimpa is similar to a humeral veil. This long, rectangular piece of white fabric is sometimes worn by those who serve as miter- or crosier-bearers when the Bishop is present.

STORAGE: The storage of vestments depends largely on how much room you have. The best way to store most vestments is not on a hanger, but rather lying flat in a large drawer. Larger sacristies are often fitted with a vestment case, which consists of wide, shallow drawers in which the vestment can be laid, unfolded, when not in use. If this is not a possibility, consider investing in some high-quality vestment hangers. These hangers are broad to help the vestment hang correctly and prevent wrinkling, and include a special attachment to hang the stole. Stoles seem to have a way of wandering off, and hanging the stole on the same hanger with the vestment can prevent this from happening.

Linens

Altar coverings may be of various colors, but the altar cloth itself is always white.[3] There are corporals also, smaller cloths which are placed on the altar, over the altar cloth, at the time of the Presentation and Preparation of the Gifts. The altar cloth can be compared to a tablecloth, covering the altar top, while the corporal is something like a placemat, a white cloth large enough to hold the chalice and paten. A corporal may be embroidered with a cross. Other linens include the purificator—a small white cloth, often with a cross embroidered on it, which is used to wipe the edge of the chalice. The sacristy is usually home to a number of hand towels as well, which are used for the washing of hands during Mass, for Baptisms, and for a variety of other rites.

The Church does not set any limitations on the kind of fabric used for the altar cloth and other altar linens, indicating only that the altar cloth should be white. But liturgical linens need to be "set aside,"[4] that is, not used for any other purpose. They also need to be "signs of our reverence."[5] In other words, the "concern for genuineness of materials"[6] that should guide the furnishing of churches also applies to the linens used at the altar. Cheap, artificial, stained, or ragged altar linens surely do little to express reverence.

In readying the altar linens each week, consider their use. Purificators are intended to be opened and *used*, to wipe the rim of the cup or chalice during Holy Communion. They should be clean and carefully pressed, but if they are so heavily starched that they can barely be unfolded, they are not serving their purpose. Save the starch for the altar cloths and the corporals!

Sacrarium

The sacrarium is a distinctive feature of a well-equipped sacristy. "The sacristy near the sanctuary will usually contain the *sacrarium*, the special sink used for the reverent disposal of sacred substances. This sink has a cover, a basin, and a special pipe and drain that empty directly into the earth, rather than into the sewer system. After Mass, when the vessels are rinsed and cleansed, the water is poured into the sacrarium so that any remaining particles that might be left will not be poured into the sewer but will go directly into the earth. When the purificators and corporals are rinsed before being washed, the water is disposed of in the sacrarium. The sacrarium also can be used to discard old baptismal water, leftover ashes, and the previous year's oils, if they are not burned.

In addition, if any of the Precious Blood is accidentally spilled during Mass, it is carefully wiped up and the area is washed. The water from this process also should be poured down the sacrarium. Reverence for sacred things continues even after they are no longer useful in the liturgy."[7]

The sacrarium should be clearly marked, and covered when not in use. Given its special nature, it should not be used except for the purposes outlined above. Thus, in addition to the sacrarium, the sacristy needs to have another sink as well, where ministers can wash their hands before and after Mass, and where day-to-day scrubbing and cleaning can take place.

Ritual Books

Books continue to be central to our worship today. Our most important books are *The Roman Missal* and the *Lectionary for Mass*. *The Roman Missal* contains the prayers of the Mass such as the Penitential Act, the Collect, the Eucharistic Prayer, the concluding prayers—everything the priest says, in short, except the readings, the homily, and the Prayer of the Faithful (Universal Prayer).[8] The Lectionary contains the readings of the day. Depending on which edition is used in your parish, the Lectionary is usually divided into several volumes. Most often, you can expect to find the Sunday and weekday readings in different volumes (the weekday readings are usually in two separate books, for Year I and Year II). Another volume will contain the readings for ritual and votive Masses (this is where you would look for the readings for Confirmations, weddings, or funerals). And there is often also a *Book of the Gospels*, which contains only the readings of the Gospel for Sundays, solemnities, and feasts of the Lord.

The Church has an abundance of other ritual books as well, all of which the sacristan needs to have some familiarity with. These include (in no particular order) the *Liturgy of the Hours*, the *Rite of Christian Initiation of Adults*, the *Order of Christian Funerals*, the *Rite of Marriage*, the *Pastoral Care of the Sick: Rites of Anointing and Viaticum*, the *Rite of Penance*, the *Book of Blessings*, the *Order for the Solemn Exposition of the Holy Eucharist*, and *Sunday Celebrations in the Absence of a Priest*, among others. As if this were not enough, there are other Lectionaries to familiarize yourself with—a *Lectionary for Mass* (and *The Sacramentary for*

Masses in Honor of the Blessed Virgin Mary) and a *Lectionary for Masses with Children,* with readings for Sunday and weekdays. And there is usually a local Ordo as well, an annual calendar that gives information on the liturgy of each day, including the readings, the saints, the liturgical color, as well as information on the Liturgy of the Hours.

A good way to get comfortable with these resources is to spend some time exploring the table of contents of each ritual book. It sounds obvious, but it really helps. The more time you spend exploring these books, the less daunting they will seem.

Ritual books should be handled with care and reverence, put away following each liturgical celebration and stored in an appropriate place. They should be easily accessible, especially those that get the most use— the *Lectionary for Mass, The Roman Missal,* and the *Book of the Gospels.* They should also be dignified and worthy in their binding and in their condition.[9]

Candles

The sacristy usually houses a variety of candles. Candles are a sign of the presence of the risen Christ in our midst. Thus candles are carried with the cross and the *Book of the Gospels* in the Entrance Procession. Candles are lit around the altar during the celebration of the Mass. A candle burns before the Blessed Sacrament to mark Christ's presence in the eucharistic bread reserved there, and during exposition candles burn around the exposed sacrament.

Many of the rites of the Church feature candles. A lit candle is presented to the newly baptized, a symbol of the light of Christ, and at funerals the lighting of the Paschal candle is a reminder of the Resurrection. On February 2, the feast of the Presentation of the Lord, the entire assembly carries lit candles, and during the Rites for the Dedication of a Church the lighting of candles on the altar and of special candles on the walls of the church is a "sign of rejoicing."[10] And the office of Evening Prayer often includes a *lucernarium,* or lighting of candles.

In many churches, candles are also lit before icons or images of saints. It's true that the sacristan's life would be considerably easier without candles—they need constant maintenance and constant replenishing, and nothing can make a mess like an unruly candle. But candles are important. In fact, they're indispensable. We need these visible, tangible symbols; they speak to us in ways that words cannot fully express. See pages 67 for ideas about keeping candles and candleholders clean, and removing wax from various surfaces.

Incense

Incense is carried in procession, and it is used to incense sacred things such as the altar, the cross, the *Book of the Gospels*, the priest, the assembly, and the consecrated bread and wine. In the liturgy, incense directs our attention to the holy, to the presence of God.

Incense is usually a combination of organic materials, which when burned release a fragrant aroma. These can consist of aromatic gums from trees—frankincense and myrrh fall into this category. But some woods and barks, seeds, fruits, and flowers can be burned as incense as well. And there are dozens of incense blends on the market that include artificial colors and scents.

> ✠ "Thurification or incensation is an expression of reverence and of prayer. . . ."
> —*GIRM, 276*

With all the options available, it is hard to know what kind of incense to use. In general, all-natural products are best. Experiment to find the best blend of oily (resins like frankincense) and dry materials. Keep track of the complaints you get to see which blends minimize the coughing. And keep in mind that some people have serious allergic reactions to incense, while others just don't like it. "Hypo-allergenic" incense blends are available, but it is impossible to produce smoke without putting particulate matter into the air. Some parishes designate one portion of the church an "incense-free zone," where smoke doesn't reach when incense is used at Mass. Others have a particular Mass each weekend where incense is never used, so that those with severe allergies or sensitivity to incense have some options.

Maintenance and Housekeeping

In addition to all of the items used for the Mass itself, many other items are needed in a well-supplied sacristy. A good quantity of soft cloths should be on hand for the washing, drying, and polishing of the various vessels. And a supply of rags should be handy for heavy-duty cleaning jobs. The sacristy will also need a range of other cleaning supplies. Metal polish, wood polish, and wax remover for the various surfaces; a gentle dishwashing soap for the sacred vessels; an iron and ironing board, spray starch and stain remover for the linens, a sewing kit for basic repairs to albs and other vestments; a vacuum, broom, and dustpan.

You will find some ideas for cleaning various surfaces on pages 66–68. But keep your ears open and talk with the other sacristans in your church—much valuable lore on what works on this candleholder or that ciborium, this vestment or that marble statue, is handed down from sacristan to sacristan.

Sound and Lighting Systems

In some churches, sound and lighting systems are as simple as flipping a switch, but in more and more churches there is increased flexibility for both sound and light—and that makes for greater complexity as well. Take time to familiarize yourself with the sound and lighting systems, and know what the options are. Where is the sound system turned on and off? Are there power switches only on the main sound board, or on the microphones themselves as well? Is it possible to adjust the volume on the individual microphones based on who is speaking, or is it "one-size-fits-all"? What is the ideal distance from microphone to the person speaking? Is there a lavaliere or handheld microphone for the priest, lector or reader, or cantor? If so, how often does the battery need to be changed? Where is the best place to clip the microphone? Vestments can sometimes create challenges for pinning the priest's lavaliere microphone on correctly. Figure out the best place for the microphone by testing it in advance, rather than by trial and error during the liturgy itself.

How flexible is the lighting? Work with those who prepare the liturgical environment to ensure that the lighting levels are adequate and appropriate to the season. It's important to be able to turn the lights on; but at certain key moments—like the Easter Vigil—it's equally important to be able to turn the lights off. Newer lighting systems often have features that allow for gentle variations in lighting, and smooth fades in turning the lights up or down. Used in moderation, such systems can add to the beauty of the celebration and help the community enter into the liturgical time.

Security and Other Concerns

Because the parish office is usually not open on Sunday, the sacristy also serves, in some ways, as an office or "headquarters" on weekends. Often, the collection is kept here in a locking cupboard or vault over the weekend, and that means that the sacristy needs to be safe and secure.

The sacristy should be equipped with a telephone and answering machine or voice mail so that calls can be made in and out in case of emergency. Keep a parish directory on hand, as well as emergency contact information for all liturgical ministers, especially children. The sacristy should also have a fire extinguisher and first aid kit. Many parishes now also keep a defibrillator, and designate volunteers and staff members who are trained to use it. Basic emergency training is simple to arrange through your local fire department, and it can truly save a life.

A Walk through the Church

As we have seen in the brief overview of the sacristy, the sacristan's role has to do with the sacred: in particular with the holy things of worship, the vessels, linens, vestments, and other objects necessary for the celebration of the liturgy. The church building itself is the most important of these holy things.

The Church Building

The church building is an image of an invisible reality, a metaphor, as it were, for the holy people of God. It is both *domus Dei,* the house of God, and *domus ecclesiae,* the house of the Church.[11] The exterior of the church invites all to come and experience what is within. Towers, spires, and domes are visible from a long way off, and constitute a visual invitation and reminder. Bells ring out a call to prayer, recollection, or rejoicing to the broader community—to those without, rather than those within. Doors invite all to enter. Vestibules or entryways provide a transition between the world without and the world within. The main body of the church indicates at once what the building is for: not an auditorium or performance hall, but a place where the community gathers to carry out the liturgy. The church building sets aside a space for worship, in the same way that the liturgy sets aside a time for worship.[12]

The Nave

The main body of the church, where the assembly gathers, is sometimes called the nave (the word comes from the Latin word for *ship*, and refers to its shape). Because the primary function of a church is to serve the needs of the liturgy and to foster the assembly's participation,[14] the nave is an important part of the church. It should be so arranged as to encourage the active participation of the assembly and to ensure that processions, including the sprinkling and incensation of the assembly, can take place in a worthy way. Given the importance of the assembly's participation, the chairs or pews deserve careful attention. Is the place for the assembly welcoming and dignified? Are the pews or chairs dusted and tidy? Are the hymnals or worship aids in good condition, ready to be used? Are offering envelopes readily available? Are there places in the assembly for those in wheelchairs or with other disabilities?

The Sanctuary

The sanctuary is distinguished from the rest of the church, without being starkly separated from it.

THE ALTAR: "The altar on which is effected the Sacrifice of the Cross made present under sacramental signs, is also the table of the Lord to which the People of God is convoked to participate in the Mass, and it is also the center of thanksgiving that is accomplished through the Eucharist."[14]

> ✛ In accordance with traditional custom, near the tabernacle a special lamp, fueld by oil or wax, should shine permanently to indicate the presence of Christ and honor it.
> —GIRM, 316

The focal point of the sanctuary—indeed, the focal point of the entire church building—is the altar. No matter what the architectural style of your church, the altar should be the undisputed center and focal point of the building. It should not be obscured by candlesticks, flowers, poorly ironed linens, or awkwardly dangling microphone cords. Remove dead flowers promptly and be sure lighting on the altar is adequate not only during Mass, but whenever the church is open for prayer.

THE AMBO: The ambo is another privileged place in the church building, located in the sanctuary. The meaning of the ambo should be understood in the context of the celebration of the Eucharist. "Here the

✛ "The central focus of the area in which the word of God is proclaimed during the liturgy is the *ambo*. The design of the ambo and its prominent placement reflects the dignity and nobility of that saving word and draws the attention of those present to the proclamation of the word."
—*Built of Living Stones*, 61

Christian community encounters the living Lord in the word of God and prepares itself for the 'breaking of the bread' and the mission to live the word that will be proclaimed."[15] In newer churches, there is often a visual connection between the ambo and the altar, between the table of God's word and the table of the Lord's Body and Blood.

Keep the ambo dusted, tidy, and ready for use. If there is a shelf inside the ambo, do not use it to store items except during Mass. Be sure to clear out this area on a regular basis—it should not become a refuge for glasses of water, pencils, post-it notes, old homilies, and the Prayer of the Faithful from two weeks ago. Because it is the table of the word, it should be kept as clean and ready as a table at home where a banquet is about to be served.

✛ The chair of the Priest Celebrant must signify his function of presiding over the gathering and of directing the prayer.
—GIRM, 310

THE PRESIDENTIAL CHAIR: The presidential chair is located in the sanctuary. Although "any appearance of a throne is to be avoided,"[16] the presidential chair should be different from the other chairs in the church. Even when empty, it should speak to the special role of the minister who uses it. It should be clearly visible and free from clutter.

Adjacent to the presidential chair, or at least placed in relation to it, are the chairs for other ministers—in particular the deacon and any concelebrating priests. The arrangement of chairs for other ministers should "be arranged so that they are clearly distinguishable from seats for the clergy and so that the ministers are easily able to carry out the function entrusted to them."[17]

THE CREDENCE TABLE: The credence table is usually placed in the sanctuary as well. The term comes from the Italian word, still in use, *credenza*, meaning simply a buffet or shelf. This table should be large enough to hold the various vessels needed for the Mass—the chalice and paten, cups, and plates for the distribution of Eucharist, and so on.

The credence table should be considered a holy place as well, and should not be used for other things, such as drinking water, musical instruments, or stacks of hymnals. The credence table is usually covered with a cloth before any of the sacred vessels are placed on it. Following the Communion Rite, the credence table may also used for the purification of the vessels.

The tabernacle and sanctuary lamp may be located in the sanctuary or in a separate chapel.

TABERNACLE AND SANCTUARY LAMP: The tabernacle and sanctuary lamp may be located in the sanctuary, or in a separate chapel, but certain principles apply everywhere. The tabernacle itself should be kept locked.[18] The consecrated hosts inside should be kept in a covered, opaque vessel or ciborium, made of worthy materials.[19] These hosts should be kept fresh by being continually replenished. The place of the tabernacle—whether in the sanctuary or in a separate chapel—should be "truly noble, prominent, conspicuous, worthily decorated, and suitable for prayer."[20] For the sacristan, that means ensuring that the chapel is accessible, tidy, well-lit, and inviting. If you provide prayer books or other aids to meditation, they should be checked every day to ensure that they are neatly arranged, and that they do not get dog-eared or outdated. The tabernacle itself (depending, of course, on what materials it is made of) will need regular dusting, inside and out, as well as a thorough cleaning on occasion. The ciboria and any linens or veils used inside or outside the tabernacle should be neat and well-maintained.

> ✚ "In accordance with traditional custom, near the tabernacle a special lamp, fueled by oil or wax, should be kept alight to indicate and honor the presence of Christ."
>
> —GIRM, 316

The tabernacle should always be kept locked, and the key in a secure location. [21] Only those who need access to the tabernacle should have access to the tabernacle.

The sanctuary lamp serves a practical function—it is an indication to the faithful that the Blessed Sacrament is reserved in the tabernacle. But it also is meant to "indicate the presence of Christ,"[22] and so it should be genuine and carefully maintained. What is the regular pattern for replacing the candle or refilling the lamp? It is good to have a weekly routine, rather than waiting until someone notices that the candle is out! A good time to replace it might be just before the church closes on Friday evening. That way, the people who come for the Sunday Masses will see a fresh candle, burning brightly, rather than the last flickerings of a once-lovely light.

The Baptistry

For most of the year, the Paschal candle stands near the baptismal font, and is lit for Baptisms as well as for funerals. The Paschal candle is a sign of Christ not only during Easter Time, but throughout the year, and for that reason it should be kept clean and always ready to use. If your parish has a baptistry that is separate from the main body of the church (for example, off the vesti-bule), do not allow this space to double as storage area for folding chairs or notice boards or anything else. Even when not in use, the baptistry serves as a reminder of Baptism to all who come to the church, and it should look alive.

> ✠ "It is customary to locate the baptismal font either in a special area within the main body of the church or in a separate baptistry. Through the waters of baptism the faithful enter the life of Christ. For this reason the font should be visible and accessible to all who enter the church building."
> —BLS, 67

The water in the font, as in any stoups or holy water vessels at the entrances of the church, should be fresh, abundant, and inviting.

Is the holy water available in the church truly a reminder of the grace of Baptism, or is it stingy in quantity, slimy, or, worse yet, green? When a font needs cleaning, empty the blessed water into the sacrarium and refill it from the blessed water in the baptismal font. If your parish celebrates the sacrament of Baptism on a regular basis, you might sched-ule the cleaning of the fonts before each Baptism, since the rite includes the blessing of water.

> ✠ "The water used in baptism should be true water and, both for the sake of authentic sacramental symbolism and for hygienic reasons, should be pure and clean. The baptis-mal font . . . should be spotlessly clean and of pleasing design."
> —*Christian Initiation*, General Introduction, 18–19

THE AMBRY: The ambry, the place where the oil of catechumens, the oil of the sick, and the chrism are kept, is often located near the baptistry, because two of these oils are used in the rites of Christian initiation.[23] "Since bright light or high temperatures can hasten spoilage, parishes will want to choose a location that helps to preserve the freshness of the oil."[24] As with the tabernacle, the place where the oils are kept should be "simple, dignified, and secure."[25] Oils should be kept in sealed containers to keep out dust. At the end of the year, the sacristan is usually responsible for the disposal of any leftover sacred oils. They may be poured into the sacrarium, buried in the earth, or burned.

Vestibule, Narthex, or Gathering Place

Many church buildings are also equipped with a vestibule, narthex, or gathering place. These areas require the sacristan's attention as well. The vestibule is the first part of the church people see as they arrive. Is it dark, musty, and littered with brochures and old church bulletins? The vestibule should be well-lit, clean, and welcoming—a space in which to transition from the busy world outside to the consecrated space within. The vestibule (like the sacristies) is part of the church building, and at times it serves a liturgical function as well. For example, in many parishes the narthex is used for viewings before the funeral liturgy begins. This space should therefore be maintained with the same care as the sanctuary itself.

Confessional or Reconciliation Chapel

The confessionals or reconciliation chapel, especially if they are not used every day, may sometimes be considered for storage spaces. But resist the temptation to store hymnals or microphone stands or any other good and needful items in the confessionals when they are not in use. Here's a general rule of thumb: if it is *ever* used as a confessional, it should *never* be used as a closet. If the confessional is never used, it would be better to remove it than to convert it into a closet. The confessionals or Reconciliation chapel should have a welcoming atmosphere. A simple flower arrangement can work wonders.

Side or Devotional Chapels

Most churches have side chapels or devotional chapels of various kinds and sizes. Like the Blessed Sacrament chapel and the place for the sacrament of Reconciliation, these chapels need regular maintenance. If candles burn before the images of the saints, the candles should be genuine, not electric. They should be well-stocked whenever the church is open, so that people can easily light a candle as they offer a prayer. The offering boxes should be emptied regularly, and any signage about the suggested donation for candles should be worded with care. Wherever there is wax there is mess, so sacristans should be prepared to spend quite a bit of time cleaning and maintaining candles.

No matter how grand and beautiful your church building is, if it is dark and cold, with burnt-out lights here and there, dusty pews filled with outdated worship aids, and grimy fonts, it will feel neglected and unloved. And no matter how humble your church is, if people come in to a welcoming place, with current bulletins neatly arranged, fonts filled with fresh water, tidy pews, fresh flowers and plants, and candles burning before the images of the saints, they will know at once that they have walked into a living—and lived in—house of worship.

Preparing for Mass

This is an overview of the preparations for Mass. Keep in mind that there are variations in every faith community, and be sure to consult with your pastor, and with those in your parish who coordinate the liturgy and prepare the liturgical environment, about local practice.

Opening the Church

The sacristan is often the person responsible for opening the church building before the first liturgy of the day. That means that to be the sacristan is also to be a minister of hospitality. When people come into the church, the church should be ready for them: lights on, heat, air-conditioning/fans running, restrooms freshly cleaned and stocked with all necessary supplies, and so on. If time permits, it is a good idea to turn on the sound system and check the microphones before the building opens. That way, you won't have to interrupt the prayer of the people with "testing, one, two, three." If any seats need to be reserved, put out the signs before the church opens (or at least well before the liturgy begins).

It's best to unlock all of the church doors, even double doors. When you open the doors of the church, be prepared to smile. Very often, the sacristan is the first person people see as they arrive: the way you welcome them can make a big difference.

Check the Ordo

Begin your preparations for the liturgy by determining what day it is in the liturgical calendar. LTP's *Sourcebook for Sundays, Seasons, and Weekdays: The Almanac for Pastoral Liturgy* is a good place to begin—it includes the liturgical color for each day, the Lectionary number of the readings, as well as information about solemnities, feasts, and other commemorations. You should consult your local Ordo as well for any variations in your diocese. See also page 72 for more information.

Preparing the Vestments

If space permits, lay out the vestment to make it easy for the priest to get ready. The vestments should be arranged in the order the priest will put them on. Thus, the sacristan should begin with the chasuble, which is the last of the vestments the priest will put on. Lay it face down, and arrange the stole on top of it. On top of the stole, lay the priest's alb, again face down, folding up the bottom so he can slip into it easily. If the priest uses an amice (this depends on the cut of the alb), this should be laid out on top of the alb. If he uses a cincture (again, this depends on his alb and his custom) the cincture is placed under the alb because he will need to put on the alb first.

Vestments for the deacon can be laid out in the same way, again, as space permits: dalmatic, then stole, with the alb on top.

If the priest or deacon needs to wear a microphone, place the microphone with the vestments. Similarly, if the priest will need a hymnal for the Entrance Chant, place it (marked with the appropriate song of the day) with his vestments. Otherwise, place it near his chair before Mass begins.

Vestments for lay ministers should be prepared in advance, too. If you have a number of servers or acolytes, have their albs hanging clean and ready for when they arrive. If albs are not assigned to the servers by name or number, hang them in order of length, so that the servers can easily find an alb that fits them. The vesture for lay ministers, as for the clergy, should be checked each week to ensure that it is clean and ready for the Sunday liturgy.

Prepare the Ritual Books

Next prepare the ritual books. Here's a detailed explanation on how to do this.

OVERVIEW OF THE ROMAN MISSAL: *The Roman Missal* is a new edition, and a new translation, of the book we formerly called *The Sacramentary*. For the most part, the book is organized in the same way, but just enough has changed to keep sacristans on their toes! Hopefully the following outline will help you to navigate your way through this freshly translated edition of our most important collection of liturgical prayers. At the beginning of *The Roman Missal,* you will find a series of official documents, including the *Apostolic Constitution* of Pope Paul VI, published with first edition of the renewed Roman Missal in 1969. Next in the volume is the *General Instruction of the Roman Missal,* which is often printed and referred to as if it were a separate document—really, it is an introduction to this book, and provides detailed rubrics and explanations of the hows and whys of the Roman Catholic liturgy.

After the *General Instruction,* you will find the *Universal Norms on the Liturgical Year and the General Roman Calendar,* which offers an outline of the liturgical year. You might take special note of the "Table of Liturgical Days according to their order of precedence," which provides a ranking of all the observances of the liturgical year.

Then you will find the *General Roman Calendar,* which includes saints' days, holy days, and their rank (optional memorial, memorial, feast, solemnity). While your local Ordo will provide you with the most complete information on observances, it's good to know that you have this calendar at your fingertips as well.

The *General Roman Calendar* concludes the introductory matter in *The Roman Missal.* Following this document, the primary content of *The Roman Missal*—the liturgical texts for the celebration of the Eucharist throughout the year —begins with the Proper of Time (formerly called the Proper of Seasons). "Proper" refers to prayers that are specific to a particular occasion—here, to the "Time" of the year. In the Proper of Time you find the prayers for the Sundays and weekdays of Advent, Christmas Time, Lent, the Paschal Triduum, Easter Time, and Ordinary Time. The Proper of Time ends with the "Solemnities of the Lord during the Ordinary Time," which include The Most Holy Trinity, the Most Holy Body and Blood of Christ (*Corpus Christi*), the Most

Sacred Heart of Jesus, and the Solemnity of Our Lord Jesus Christ, King of the Universe.

One change is to be noted in the Proper of Time. Formerly, all the Prefaces were located together, within the Order of Mass. Now, proper Prefaces can be found with the prayers of the day. This includes the Prefaces for the Baptism of the Lord, the Sundays of Lent, Pentecost, and the Solemnities of the Lord during Ordinary Time. The majority of the other Prefaces are still found within the Order of Mass (some, such as the solemnity of the Immaculate Conception of the Blessed Virgin Mary are found in the Proper of Saints).

After the Proper of Time comes the Order of Mass, the section of *The Roman Missal* that is used at all times of the year. This section is set apart by tabs, to make it easy for the priest to find his way from the Order of Mass to the Prefaces and Eucharistic Prayers.

This section of *The Roman Missal* is organized in the order the different elements are used at Mass. The Order of Mass begins with the Introductory Rites—the greeting, the Penitential

> *As a general rule of thumb, you'll find "fixed feasts," those which always occur on the same day of the calendar, in the Proper of Saints, while "movable feasts" such as Easter are found in the Proper of Time. But this is not always the case, Nativity of the Lord being the most notable exception. Although it always occurs on December 25, it is found in the Proper of Time.*

Act, the Gloria, the dialogues and prayers for the Liturgy of the Word, and the Creed. Then comes the Preface Dialogue, followed by fifty Prefaces for the feasts and seasons of the year. Note that the six Prefaces for weekdays have not disappeared: they are now called "Common Prefaces."

Following the Prefaces come the Eucharistic Prayers, marked by tabs. The new translation of *The Roman Missal* collects in one place several texts which were formerly published as appendices, or in separate volumes. These include the "Order of Mass with the Participation of a Single Minister," the two Eucharistic Prayers for Reconciliation, which formerly appeared at the end of the book, and the four Eucharistic Prayers for Use in Masses for Various Needs. This new arrangement makes these Eucharistic Prayers much more accessible than before, opening up more of the resources of *The Roman Missal* for the priest.

Following the Eucharistic Prayers, the Order of the Mass continues with the prayers of the Communion Rite, and a wide range of Solemn Blessings and Prayers over the People.

While some appendices have been incorporated into the main body of the book, some other elements that we are used to seeing in the Order of Mass are now found in appendices. These include the Rite for the Blessing and Sprinkling of Water, which is used especially during Easter Time. These texts are now found in Appendix II. The sample invocations for the Penitential Act, which can still be composed for the local community, are now found in Appendix VI. These texts are found in the Appendix simply because that is where they are in the Latin edition of *The Roman Missal*. Their placement does not mean that they are not recommended for use! Mark them with a ribbon and use them just as you did before.

After the conclusion of the Order of Mass comes the next major section, the Proper of Saints. This includes Collects, and sometimes also Prayers over the Gifts and Prayers after Communion, for the saints of the liturgical year, from January through December. (As a general rule of thumb, you'll find "fixed feasts," those which always occur on the same day of the calendar, in the Proper of Saints, while "movable feasts" such as Easter are found in the Proper of Time. This is not always the case, Christmas being the most notable exception. Though it always occurs on December 25, it is found in the Proper of Time.)

The next four sections in *The Roman Missal* provide prayers for a variety of different occasions. Commons are prayers for memorials that do not have "proper" prayers. This section includes the Common of the Dedication of a Church (including prayers used on the anniversary of dedication), Common of the Blessed Virgin Mary, Common of Martyrs, of Pastors, of Doctors of the Church, of Virgins, and of Holy Men and Women. These are regularly used for the memorials of saints, which often have only a proper Collect.

The Ritual Masses are prayers for Masses at which a special rite is celebrated, whether a rite from the *Rite of Christian Initiation of Adults*, Baptism, Confirmation, conferral of Holy Orders (Ordination) or Viaticum. In this section you will also find the prayers for the wedding Mass, wedding anniversaries, and religious profession. Many of the Prefaces for the ritual Masses are now found with the other prayers for the Mass—when using these Masses, be sure you know where the Preface is!

The Masses and Prayers for Various Needs and Occasions are a wonderful resource. As the name of this section suggests, they include a wide variety of prayers for many different circumstances. There are prayers for the Church, for the Pope, for the unity of Christians, for vocations, for peace and justice, for productive land, for rain, for prisoners, and for many other "needs and occasions." The third edition of *The Roman Missal* includes a new Mass for use in the United States, "For Giving Thanks to God for the Gift of Human Life." These prayers can be used on January 22, the anniversary of the Supreme Court decision Roe v. Wade, or at other times of the year, as permitted. In the next section are found the Votive Masses. "Votive Masses of the mysteries of the Lord or in honor of the Blessed Virgin Mary or of the Angels or of any given Saint or of all the Saints may be said in response to the devotion of the faithful on weekdays in Ordinary Time, even if an optional memorial occurs." [26] Votive Masses are different from Masses for Various Needs and Occasions in that they are not directed towards a specific need; rather, they honor a mystery, like the Holy Trinity, the Holy Cross, the Holy Eucharist, or a person, like Mary, Joseph, the Apostles, Peter or Paul.

Towards the end of *The Roman Missal* we find the prayers for Masses for the Dead, including the prayers used at Funeral Masses, prayers for the anniversary of death, and prayers for all the dead and for specific needs.

The appendices are not to be overlooked, either. They include Various Chants for the Order of Mass, including chant settings for the Greeting, the Penitential Act, and the Blessing, as well as Presidential Tones for the chanting of the Collects and the readings. Credo III, the most familiar Gregorian setting of the Creed, can be found here as well, along with the musical setting of the Easter Proclamation and the Christmas Proclamation. As mentioned above, the Rite for the Blessing and Sprinkling of Water is now found in Appendix II, and the Invocations for the Penitential Act in Appendix VI. Appendix III is a new addition to the third edition of *The Roman Missal*, a Rite of Deputing a Minister to Distribute Holy Communion on a Single Occasion, for those times when insufficient priests and commissioned ministers are available.

Appendix IV includes the Rite of Blessing a Chalice and a Paten within Mass, which is also found in the Book of Blessings. "Examples of Formularies for the Universal Prayer" (Prayer of the Faithful) are found in Appendix IV. These examples may be used as they are; they can also serve as models for those entrusted with the task of writing the petitions for the parish. There are several general formulas, plus examples for every time of the liturgical year.

MARKING THE ROMAN MISSAL: How do you mark *The Roman Missal?* Again, your local Ordo will point you in the right direction. Let's take a couple of examples.

- It's the Second Sunday of Advent. Use one ribbon to mark the "proper" prayers, that is, the prayers unique to this day in the liturgical calendar. You will find them at the beginning of *The Roman Missal*, in the Proper of Time. Use another ribbon to mark the Preface. You'll find the Prefaces in the center of *The Roman Missal* within the Order of Mass. There are two Advent Prefaces. Notice that the second is used only from December 17 to 24. That means you'll want to mark Preface I of Advent for today.

The sacristan prepares to mark the proper readings in the Lectionary for Mass.

What else should be marked in *The Roman Missal?* It depends on local custom and the needs of the priest. It may be that another ribbon could be used to mark the Penitential Act for the day, either the *Confiteor,* or perhaps one of the sets of invocations found in Appendix VI. Some priests like to have the prayers for the preparation of the altar marked as well. You'll find those at the center of *The Roman Missal,* just after the Creed. (A helpful hint: fold the ribbons you are not using and tuck them out of sight, leaving visible only the ribbons that will be used during the current Mass. This will help prevent unnecessary flipping of pages.)

- It's June 5, the memorial of Saint Boniface. You find his prayers in Proper of Saints for June 5. But you notice right away that only one prayer, the Collect, is provided. So after you mark that page, you'll want to mark the rest of the prayers in one of the Commons. A note suggests using either the Common of Martyrs: For One Martyr or the Common of Pastors: For Missionaries, because Saint Boniface was a missionary who carried the Gospel to the people of Germany. You might mark both of them, and let the priest decide which set he prefers.

Having marked the prayers, you next need to mark the Preface. Again, there are two options—you can mark one of the two Prefaces of Holy Martyrs or the Preface of Holy Pastors.

• It's the Third Sunday of Lent, and the First Scrutiny of the Elect is being celebrated. There are two options for the prayers. You can mark the Prayers for the Third Sunday of Lent in the Proper of Time, or you can mark the prayers for the Scrutinies in the section Ritual Masses. Either set of prayers may be used when a Scrutiny is celebrated. Ask the priest which he prefers.

If the Scrutiny of the Elect is being celebrated in your parish, that means that the readings for Year A are being used as well. So you will want to mark the proper Preface for the Third Sunday of Lent, which is only used when the Gospel of the Woman of Samaria is read. Notice that this Preface is found in the Proper of Time, along with the other prayers for the Third Sunday of Lent. In Year B or Year C, when no Scrutiny is celebrated, one of the general Lenten Prefaces should be used. These are found in the Order of Mass.

OVERVIEW OF THE LECTIONARY FOR MASS: The Lectionary includes the readings for every day of the liturgical year, weekdays (a two-year cycle) and Sundays (a three-year cycle), readings for saints' days, readings for Ritual Masses, Votive Masses, Masses for Various Needs and Occasions, and Masses for the Dead. No wonder Lectionaries are divided into several volumes!

MARKING THE LECTIONARY: To mark the readings for a Sunday Mass, you need to know whether you are in Year A, Year B, or Year C. Here is a quick guide to the Lectionary for the next few years. Notice that the Lectionary year begins with the First Sunday of Advent, which usually falls in late November or very early December, and ends with the solemnity of Our Lord Jesus Christ, King of the Universe in late November of the following year.

	Sunday	Weekday
Advent 2012 – Christ the King 2013	Year C	I
Advent 2013 – Christ the King 2014	Year A	II
Advent 2014 – Christ the King 2015	Year B	I
Advent 2015 – Christ the King 2016	Year C	II

Once you know which year of the Lectionary you are in, it is easy to mark the Sunday Lectionary. You'll notice that every Sunday is assigned a distinctive number. This is very helpful as these numbers are unique to each set of readings. If the local Ordo tells you that the Sunday readings for today can be found at #60B, you'll find only one set of readings with that number no matter how many volumes of the Lectionary you thumb through—#60B refers to the readings for the Seventh Sunday of Easter in Year B.

After marking the Sunday Lectionary for the readers, you'll want to mark the *Book of the Gospels* for the deacon or priest. The number you used to find the readings in the Sunday Lectionary will help you find the appropriate Gospel as well.

It is helpful to place the Lectionary in a consistent place in the sacristy where the readers can review it before Mass. They will have prepared for their reading at home, but it is always good for them to see the words on the actual page they will be reading from. After the readers have had a chance to look at the Lectionary, the book can be placed at the ambo. The *Book of the Gospels* should similarly be placed where the priest or deacon can review the reading before Mass.[27]

MARKING THE WEEKDAY READINGS: The weekday readings are on a two year cycle—Year I and Year II. As a general rule of thumb, the readings for Year I are read in odd calendar years, and Year II in even calendar years. Keep in mind, though, that the liturgical year begins with Advent, so that you will move into Year I at the end of an even year, like 2012, and then back into Year II toward the end of 2013.

During Advent, Christmas Time, Lent, and Easter Time, the weekday readings are the same in both Year I and Year II. During Ordinary Time, the Gospel is the same but the First Reading and the Responsorial Psalm are different. Note also that the Lectionary numbers don't always help you here. If you go to #379, you will find the readings and Psalms for both Year I and Year II. Double-check the Ordo to find out whether you want the story of Hagar (Year I) from the book of Genesis or the harsh words of the prophet Amos (Year II)! Most Lectionaries will provide additional help by indicating Year I or Year II in the heading before the First Reading and Responsorial Psalm. Here are some examples to help you navigate through the Lectionary.

- It is the Fourth Sunday of Lent in Year B. The parish is celebrating the Second Scrutiny of the elect. When the Scrutinies are celebrated, the readings for Year A are used, no matter what year it is. That means that instead of marking #32B, you'll mark #31A in the Sunday Lectionary. You'll also mark the Gospel of the man born blind in the *Book of the Gospels*, also #31A.

- It is Friday of the Nineteenth Week in Ordinary Time. With the help of your local Ordo, you find Lectionary #417 quite easily. It is Year I, so you mark the reading from Joshua instead of the reading from Ezekiel.

- It is Thanksgiving Day, and the priest has chosen special readings: Isaiah 63:7–9, Psalm 138, Colossians 3:12–17, and Luke 17:11–19. How do you find these readings in the Lectionary? You could use the scripture index at the back of the book, which tells you where each scripture passage is found in the Lectionary. Referring to this index, you find that the reading from Isaiah occurs only once in the Lectionary, at #943 in "Masses for Various Needs and Occasions." Turning to #943 in the Lectionary, you discover that the priest has chosen all the readings from among the many options given for Masses "In Thanksgiving to God" under "Various Needs and Occasions." From here, it is easy to find and mark the other readings that have been chosen.

ADDITIONAL TEXTS: You have prepared *The Roman Missal* and the *Lectionary for Mass*. Are there additional texts that need to be readied for the celebration? If there is a special rite, you may need to prepare one of the ritual books. The Prayer of the Faithful will need to be ready for the priest who will introduce them, for the lector, reader, or deacon who will proclaim them, and for the musicians as well, if there is a sung response to the intercessions.

Preparing the Vessels

You have opened the church building, and prepared the vestments and books for the liturgy. Now you are ready to prepare the vessels for the celebration of the Mass. In the sacristy, you arrange the following items which will be placed on the **credence table**:

- the corporal to be placed on the altar at the Presentation and Preparation of the Gifts

- chalice, with a purificator

- the cruet containing water to be mingled with the wine

- the pitcher, basin, and towel for the washing of hands during the preparation of the gifts

- additional chalices, purificators, and ciboria for the distribution of Holy Communion to the assembly

In addition, you need to prepare the hosts and wine for the Mass. If there is to be a procession with the gifts, these will need to be placed on the offertory table in the nave when they are ready. How much to put out? Keep in mind that faithful should "receive the Lord's Body from hosts consecrated at the same Mass . . . ."[28] A good way to ensure that this happens is to count the actual number in the assembly before preparing the hosts for Mass. The ushers can often help with this. If you put out the same number of hosts as there are people in the assembly (and don't forget to count the choir and the other ministers) you will be sure to have enough for everyone.

If hosts do need to be brought from the tabernacle, a minister may do it during the sign of peace. The ciborium can be placed on the altar and the priest can add hosts to the ciboria as well as from the hosts consecrated during the Mass. This is necessary at times, especially if there are many latecomers who were not factored into the count! This is also a good way to ensure that the hosts that are reserved in the tabernacle are kept fresh. However, it's always a good rule of thumb to include a little extra.

Additional Preparations

If you are responsible for lighting the altar candles, do so 10 to 15 minutes before Mass begins. Do so slowly, reverently and quietly, genuflecting before the tabernacle, bowing before the altar. Bring a ritual candle-lighter already lit from the sacristy. Don't strike a match—or, worse yet, use a cigarette lighter—in sight of the assembly. The same goes for any other preparations you might make in the sanctuary or in the nave before the Mass begins. Prepare the processional cross and candles in the appropriate place. Keep the candles cleaned and trimmed so that they will light easily.

Weekday Masses

Preparations for weekday Masses are usually much the same as for Sunday Mass, with some variations. The liturgy is simpler. You probably won't need the *Book of the Gospels* on weekdays, and certainly the number of chalices and ciboria will be reduced, as will the number of hosts and the amount of wine. Different microphones may be used on weekdays, or no microphones at all might be needed. In some parishes Mass is celebrated in a smaller chapel on weekdays, rather than in the main nave of the church. Be aware of all the variations in your parish.

A checklist of the basic preparations you will need to make for every Mass, whether on Sunday or on a weekday, is available as a free download at www.ltp.org/resources/ELSAC_checklist.pdf.

After the Mass

The sacristan's work continues after Mass is over.

Purifying and Washing the Vessels

The purification of the vessels takes place at the end of the Communion Rite, or immediately following Mass. As the Communion Procession ends, the ministers bring the ciboria and chalices back to the designated place. The hosts are placed in the tabernacle by the appropriate minister, and any remaining Precious Blood is consumed. The appointed minister—a priest, deacon, or instituted acolyte—purifies the chalices, paten, and ciboria. Refer to page 75 for more information.

Sacristans cleanse the vessels after they have been purified.

After the vessels have been purified, they should be rinsed in the sacrarium, and then thoroughly washed with soap and warm water, rinsed, dried, and left ready for the next Mass.

The purificators, corporals, and altar cloth undergo a similar process. They should first be rinsed in the sacrarium, and then washed in the normal way. Purificators should be washed after every use; corporals and altar cloths when necessary, on a regular basis.

Other vessels, like the pitcher and basin for the hand washing, the cruet, and any carafes or pitchers used to hold the wine before it is consecrated can simply be washed in the sink. You do not need to rinse these items in the sacrarium.

Other After-Mass Responsibilities

After a major celebration in the parish community, try to spend more time in prayer and thanksgiving, both to God and to those you work and pray with, than in analyzing what mistakes you or others might have made.

The cleaning and arranging of the vessels should be the first priority after Mass. You will also need to bring the books—the *Lectionary for Mass*, *The Roman Missal*, any hymnals or ritual books left in the sanctuary—back to the sacristy. Prepare them for the next Mass. Reverently extinguish the candles with a snuffer so not to spill wax. Hang or lay out vestments appropriately. Walk through the nave to be sure that the place of the assembly is also ready for the next Mass—pick up stray bulletins, return hymnals to their holders, and raise kneelers.

Preparing for Special Rites

In the course of the year, the Church celebrates a rich array of special rites which require additional preparations. Here are some considerations for the special rites that are celebrated regularly in a parish setting. Often these will take place in the context of the Mass; in that case all the preparations for the regular celebration of Eucharist will also apply.

As you prepare for these rites, be sure to consult with your pastor and other ministers involved in the liturgy about customs in your parish.

Funerals

The *Order of Christian Funerals* includes not just the funeral Mass, but a number of other rites that can take place in the parish church as well, especially the vigil. Preparations for the vigil are quite simple. You will need the ritual text. A priest wears an alb and stole, and the cope may be used if desired.[29] The vigil takes the form of a Liturgy of the Word, so the readings will need to be prepared much as for a Mass. If there are to be reflections by friends or members of the family you may need to set up an additional microphone and lectern.

If the coffin or urn is received at the Vigil, then a vessel of holy water, branch (or aspergillum/sprinkler), and the funeral pall will need to be prepared at this time. (If these rites take place at the vigil, they are not repeated at the funeral Mass.)

The funeral Mass involves a number of special preparations.

IN THE CHURCH: Funerals usually bring a number of visitors, so be sure the nave is ready for them: kneelers up, hymnals available. Reserve enough seats for the family. Make sure their pews or chairs are neat and ready so that they can get to them easily during the Entrance Procession, without climbing over kneelers or squeezing past other guests. Work with the funeral home or funeral coordinator to place any flowers that arrive in an appropriate place. If there is a guest book, prepare a table at the entrance (or entrances) to the church, with writing materials.

IN THE SACRISTY: The ritual book, *Order of Christian Funerals*, will need to be used at the altar (note that there are different prayers for funeral Masses in Easter Time and outside Easter Time). Mark the Lectionary with the designated readings, usually chosen by the priest or liturgist in consultation with the family.

Unless the body is received at the Vigil, the liturgy begins with the reception of the urn or coffin at the door of the church, or in the narthex. The coffin (or urn) is sprinkled with holy water, a reminder of Baptism. The pall—a reminder of the white garment the deceased received on the day of Baptism—is then put in place. If the baptismal font is located near the door, you might put the branch for the sprinkling in the font itself. If this is not possible, a bowl with holy water and branch or aspergillum will need to be prepared and carried by a server in the procession or placed near the coffin before Mass begins. The pall should be neatly folded on a table at the back of the church, or even draped over a rear pew, readily accessible so that it can be gracefully placed over the coffin at the proper time.

The Paschal candle is another of the important baptismal reminders in the funeral liturgy. It remains lit throughout the Mass. If possible, it may be moved to a place near the coffin. Otherwise, other candles may be placed near the coffin.

After the entrance, the priest prays the Collect and the Mass proceeds as usual.

The funeral Mass concludes with the Rite of Commendation, which includes the incensation of the coffin (or urn). Prepare the incense ahead of time, and light the coals so that they will be ready when the time comes. A general rule of thumb: if the funeral takes place during Mass, light the coals after the homily. If it takes place as part of the Liturgy of the Word, light the coals during the First Reading.[30]

At the end of the Funeral Mass, it is customary in many places to toll the church bell. If this is possible in your parish, designate someone to toll the bell at the conclusion of the Rite of Commendation. Agree ahead of time on when the bell should begin ringing (and when it should stop). One old custom is to toll the bell once for each year of the person's life.

The Rite of Marriage

Weddings present their own challenges for the sacristan. The "Bride's Room" and "Groom's Room" (if these exist in your parish) will need to be prepared. In most parishes, these spaces get used for many other purposes, so they will need to be double-checked before the wedding liturgy. Each room will need a table, chairs, and a bathroom (or easy access to a bathroom). A full-length mirror will be appreciated. And you might also provide an anything-can-happen kit in each room, containing needles and thread, Kleenex, stain remover, and basic first aid items.

Special arrangements in the nave will depend on the practice in your parish. Some parishes place a runner down the central aisle, or use special antependia for the altar and ambo at weddings. You can be sure of having a number of visitors, so make sure the nave is tidy, with kneelers up and hymnals and worship aids ready to encourage the participation of all. Make sure the seats for the wedding party are reserved well in advance.

Weddings often require some rearranging in the sanctuary as well—many parishes have special kneelers or chairs for the bride and groom, maid of honor, and best man.

In the sacristy, some special preparations will be needed as well. Is it customary in your parish to use one particular vestment for weddings? Have it ready. The rite includes the blessing of wedding rings, with an optional sprinkling with holy water. Depending on the practice in your community, you may need to prepare a small tray or salver on which the rings will be placed, as well as a vessel of holy water and a fresh branch or aspergillum.

In preparing *The Roman Missal*, notice that there are three sets of wedding prayers from which the priest may choose. Each option includes not only the Collect, Prayer over the Gifts, and Prayer after Communion, but the Preface, the solemn Nuptial Blessing, which takes place immediately following the Lord's Prayer during the Mass, and a solemn blessing to be given at the end of Mass as well. Be sure the priest has a chance to look at the options and select the prayers before Mass begins.

If it is customary to ring the church bells after a wedding, make arrangements ahead of time to ensure that this happens. As with funerals, agree on the timing and length of the peal before Mass begins.

The Rite of Baptism

If the Rite of Baptism takes place outside of Mass, your primary area of attention will be the baptistry and font. Because the *Rite of Baptism* includes a blessing of water, this is a good time to clean the font. Pour the old water into the sacrarium, clean the font, and fill it with fresh water. If the Baptism is to be by immersion, it is good to heat the water if at all possible. Test the temperature on your arm rather than with the tips of your fingers (imagine you are testing a baby's bath water). About 98.6 degrees—body temperature—will be the ideal temperature for the water in the font.

Near the font, you will also need to prepare the holy oils: the oil of catechumens is used for the pre-baptismal anointing;[31] the anointing with chrism takes place following the Baptism. With the oils, place a cloth or towel for the priest or deacon to wipe his fingers. You will also need the shell or other vessel used for pouring (unless the Baptism is done by immersion or if the priest pours water with his hand),[32] as well as a towel for the newly baptized, and a baptismal candle.

The Paschal candle is lit before the rite begins. Have a candle-lighter handy to make it easy to take a light from the paschal candle to light the candle which will be presented to the newly baptized.

When the Rite of Baptism takes place in the context of the Sunday Mass, you will have some additional considerations. Reserve seating for the parents, the godparents, and those to be baptized. Reserve seats for family and friends near the baptismal font. Check well in advance to be sure you have sufficient towels and candles for each of the newly baptized. Check with the priest on which prayers to use. The proper texts from the Ritual Masses in *The Roman Missal* may be used on Sundays in Ordinary Time. A specific Preface is now included for those occasions.

The Rite of Confirmation

The Bishop is the ordinary minister of Confirmation. Whenever the Bishop comes to celebrate Mass in the parish, there will be a number of special considerations. The Bishop will usually use the priest celebrant's chair. If there are concelebrating priests, seating should be arranged for them in the sanctuary, as well as for the deacon or deacons who serve at the Mass. The Bishop will generally bring his zucchetto, miter, and crosier with him; a special place will need to be arranged in the sanctuary where the server can place the miter when not in use. If the crosier does not have a stand, find a place where it can safely (and reverently) be leaned when it is not in use. The prayers for the Mass of Confirmation are found in *The Roman Missal* under "Ritual Masses." Additional texts not found here are taken from the ritual book, the *Rite of Confirmation*.

The chrism is brought to the Bishop during the rite. In addition, you will need to prepare a smaller vessel into which the oil can be poured for the actual anointing with chrism during the rite. And, as always, provide implements for the Bishop to wash his hands following the anointing. Be sure to have water and lemons available.

Those to be confirmed will need a gathering space prepared. If they vest in albs or some other garment for the Rite of Confirmation, these will need to be made ready as well. Reserve seating for the candidates and their sponsors, and, if it is the custom, for their guests.

First Holy Communion

Be sure to get acquainted with the local practice before the celebration. In some places, the children will put on traditional finery—veils and white dresses or jacket and tie; in others, they wear the alb, the baptismal garment. In both cases, they will likely need a place to assemble with their families and catechists before the Mass begins.

In many places, the children renew their baptismal promises as part of the celebration; sometimes they light a candle as a reminder of their Baptism. If you prepare the candles, be sure they are equipped with bobeches to keep dripping wax off little fingers (and the church floor). During the liturgy, watchful adults should be on hand to keep the candles well away from flammable veils.

In the nave, reserve seating for the children, their parents, and catechists according to local custom. Plan the Holy Communion stations with special care, and make sure it is easy for the children to come forward in the Communion Procession. Easter Time is a good time for the celebration of First Holy Communion.

Anointing of the Sick during Mass

The preparations for the Anointing of the Sick are similar in some ways to those for Confirmation. Prepare a dignified place for the oil of the sick to be placed in the sanctuary. Prepare a dish into which the oil can be poured when it is time for the anointings (if several priests are present to assist with the anointings, prepare a dish for each of them). The dish or other vessel can be prepared ahead of time. Something resembling a beaker also works. Arrange the seating for those to be anointed, keeping in mind that some may have difficulty moving in procession. They should be seated in such a way that the priest can easily come to them. Prepare a place where the priest or priests can wash their hands after the anointings.

The Rite of Christian Initiation of Adults

Throughout the year, special rites are celebrated with those preparing for Baptism or reception into the full communion of the Catholic Church. These rites demand a variety of different preparations. For example, the Rite of Acceptance calls for a procession to the doors of the church to meet those to be admitted into the Order of Catechumens.

Is there a suitable place at the entrance of the church, where those to be received can be seen by the assembly? What special microphones will be needed? Will the responses of the catechumens need to be amplified also? Where will the signing of the catechumens take place?

The Scrutinies of the elect, which take place on the Third, Fourth, and Fifth Sundays of Lent, require special preparations as well. There needs to be room for the elect, their sponsors, and the priest who will lay hands on each of them. And because the prayer of the assembly is an important part of the rite, it is important that the people be able to see what is happening.

When the Rite of Reception into Full Communion for those already baptized in other Christian churches is celebrated in the parish community, the priest who receives the candidates also normally confirms them.[33] Where will the Confirmations take place? Before the altar? At the priest celebrant's chair? Who will hold the chrism? Where will the priest wash his hands?

In addition to these special rites, the catechumens participate in dismissals all year round. Following the homily during the Mass, they are sent forth from the community to gather in another place to reflect on the scriptures. The dismissals are an important part of their formation in the faith, and they are also a reminder that they are not yet able to remain with the assembly to celebrate the Eucharist. When the dismissal is celebrated, you may need to prepare the place where they will gather, as well as special seating for them during the Liturgy of the Word, perhaps also a special cross to lead the catechumens out of the church.

The Liturgy of the Hours

More and more parishes are celebrating the Liturgy of the Hours. Preparations are usually fairly simple, but also quite different from those for Mass.

The priest vests in an alb, stole, and, if desired, a cope. A lay presider will often wear an alb for the Liturgy of the Hours. If a special worship aid is not used, the appropriate volume of the Liturgy of the Hours will need to be marked, not only for the priest but for the reader and other ministers as well.

Sometimes the chairs or pews will be rearranged to facilitate the antiphonal singing or recitation of the Psalms. Find out what the custom is in your parish. Evening Prayer sometimes includes a procession with cross and candles, or a *lucernarium* (a ceremonial lighting of candles). If this is the case in your community, be sure the candles are prepared in advance, and light the Paschal candle before the prayer begins.

The Sacristan and the Liturgical Year

The sacristan is privileged to prepare for all the major feasts and fasts of the liturgical year. Here are some of the holy days you will want to be aware of as the liturgical year unfolds. Much will depend on your local community—consult with your pastor, liturgist, and environment committee. Is there a special processional cross, set of candles, or monstrance that is used only for Advent, Christmas Time, Lent, or Easter Time? Are there icons or other images that are arranged in the church for specific seasons or celebrations? Are different violet vestments used in Advent and Lent? Is the white or gold of Christmas Time different from that of Easter Time? Find out what the practices are in your community.

Advent and Christmas Time

Advent is a period of expectation, in which we look to the coming of Christ at the end of time, and prepare to celebrate his coming among us at Christmas Time. For the sacristan, Advent brings some significant changes. Violet vestments are worn, with the option of rose-colored vestments on the Third Sunday of Advent (called "Gaudete" Sunday because of the first word of the Entrance Antiphon—"Rejoice!"). Many parishes keep an Advent wreath in the church, usually a circle of evergreen fronds on which are set four candles, representing the four weeks of Advent. These candles will need to be maintained carefully so that they last through the whole liturgical time. If they are lit as part of the Advent Masses, be sure they are clean and easy to light. If the wreath is adorned with live branches, be sure these do not become dry. Replace them if necessary during the liturgical time.

Advent is also the time to get ready for Christmas Time. Clean the nativity figures and other ornamentals. Stock up on the supplies you will need—not only wine, hosts, candles, and incense for the Christmas liturgies, but also wire-clippers, extension cords, and whatever else will be needed to prepare the church for Christmas Time. In addition to the *Lectionary for Mass* and *The Roman Missal*, you may also need to prepare the Christmas and Epiphany Proclamations during this time. These proclamations are found in *The Roman Missal*. Keep a close eye on poinsettias, greens, trees, and other Christmas decorations. Evergreen branches can be dangerous when dry.

Ordinary Time during the Winter

This is the perfect time to prepare for Lent. If you burn last year's palms to create the ashes for Ash Wednesday, collect them from the parishioners during these weeks before Lent begins.

These weeks before Lent are also the time to get the violet vestments dry-cleaned and to dust the Stations of the Cross.

Lent

Lent begins with Ash Wednesday, which requires many special preparations. The blessing of the ashes requires a vessel of holy water and branch or aspergillum. The ashes themselves will need to be placed in small bowls, metal, porcelain, crystal, or glass. You may also want to have a number of small plastic containers on hand for ministers to carry blessed ashes to the homebound. Have a good supply of clean towels and soap in the sacristy so that those who distribute the ashes can wash their hands.

Lent brings with it a number of special devotions and rites. If the parish prays the Stations of the Cross, be sure that booklets or worship aids, if used, are available in sufficient numbers. The Scrutinies of the elect take place on the Third, Fourth, and Fifth Sundays of Lent. The elect may need special seating in the church throughout Lent.

During Lent, prepare for the liturgies of Holy Week. Order palms for Palm Sunday, if you have not already done so. Make sure you have everything you need for the celebration of the Paschal Triduum. Test the heater on the baptismal font.

Sacristans, as well as liturgists and environment committees, will want to take time during this season to review *Paschale Solemnitatis: A Circular Letter Concerning Preparing and Celebrating the Easter Feasts*, which was released by the Congregation for Divine Worship and the Discipline of the Sacraments in 1988. It is full of invaluable guidance on preparing for the Triduum in union with the whole Church.

PALM SUNDAY: Palm Sunday requires some special arrangements. How are the palms or branches distributed to the faithful? Are they handed to them as they enter, or placed in urns or other vessels? If you order your palms, order enough that you do not have to be stingy with them. Know in advance whether they will arrive ready to use or whether they will require additional preparation.

Where do the people gather for the procession of palms? That space may require some special attention also, especially if it is a gym or other gathering space not normally used for liturgy. It might be as simple as putting the basketballs away and clearing away the folding tables, or it could be that more extensive arrangements needed. Prepare in advance—don't get caught unawares on Palm Sunday morning!

Prepare for the reading (or chanting) of the Passion. If the reading is divided among several voices, you may need to prepare special microphones with music stands or lecterns. Place the readings in good quality binders.

The Paschal Triduum

This is the shortest and the most important season of the liturgical year. The liturgies of these three days are demanding. Prepare in advance to ensure that the transitions between these very different liturgies happen smoothly and without stress.

HOLY THURSDAY: During the day, the Blessed Sacrament is removed from the tabernacle by the appropriate minister, and the lamp is extinguished. Leave the doors of the tabernacle open so that people can see at a glance that it is empty. Any remaining consecrated hosts are kept in a different place—often the sacristy—during the Triduum. Prepare this place in advance—a locking cupboard is ideal. Let people know that the Blessed Sacrament is reserved there by placing a candle in front of that cupboard, or in some other way.

Prepare the vestments well in advance. If possible, use a simpler white today than you will use on Easter Sunday.

In many parishes, the newly blessed and consecrated oils are carried in procession on Holy Thursday. You can find the Order for the Reception of the Holy Oils in the *Sourcebook for Sundays, Seasons, and Weekdays: The Almanac for Pastoral Liturgy.* Clean and prepare the ambry to receive these new oils. Reverently discard the old oils by pouring them down the sacrarium or burying them in the ground. The new oils should never be mixed with the old oils.

Prepare for the washing of feet. Be sure you have sufficient basins, pitchers, and towels available. Where will those to have their feet washed be seated? Do specific seats need to be reserved for them in the nave? Do stools or chairs need to be prepared? Prepare in advance.

Holy Communion should be given under both kinds today, if possible. Count the assembly carefully to ensure that enough bread and wine is prepared for the assembly for this night and enough bread consecrated for reservation and distribution of Holy Communion on Good Friday.

Ready the "altar of repose," the place for Holy Thursday adoration. (If the Blessed Sacrament is normally located in a chapel separate from the main altar, this chapel may be used for the Holy Thursday adoration.) Work with the liturgical environment committee to ensure that the altar of repose is fittingly decorated. Double-check that the route of the eucharistic procession is clear and easy to navigate.

Be prepared for the stripping of the altar after Mass. Remove flowers, candles, altar cloth, and any other decorations. This should be done quietly and reverently.

Adoration of the Blessed Sacrament can continue until, but not past, midnight. At midnight, the ciborium containing the hosts for Holy Communion on Good Friday should be removed to a secure place (usually in the sacristy).

GOOD FRIDAY: Before the church opens in the morning, be sure that the Blessed Sacrament has been transferred to the sacristy, and any flowers and candles have been removed. No candles should be lit at the shrines of the saints today. The fonts should be empty.

The Celebration of the Lord's Passion is the principal liturgy today. Prepare red vestments. Even though the liturgy tonight is not a Mass, the chasuble is worn. The Passion according to John is read or chanted—the lectors, readers, or cantors will each need a copy of the text. Prepare the Cross for adoration. Prepare the candles that will be placed around the altar for Holy Communion. Prepare the linens and vessels for the Communion Rite. *The Roman Missal* indicates that a humeral veil be worn when the Blessed Sacrament is brought to the altar for communion on Good Friday.

HOLY SATURDAY: This is a day of busy preparations for the Easter Vigil, the most important liturgy of the liturgical year. Be sure you have enough help to decorate the church for Easter. Have a box of supplies ready to go, including fishing line, wire, scissors, tape, floral shears, and any other supplies that might come in handy for the preparation of the environment.

The Easter fire should be the real thing. "Insofar as possible, a suitable place should be prepared outside the church for the blessing of the new fire, whose flames should be such that they genuinely dispel the darkness and light up the night."[34]

Prepare the Paschal candle, "which for effective symbolism must be made of wax, never be artificial, be renewed each year, be only one in number, and be of sufficiently large size so that it may evoke the truth that Christ is the light of the world."[35]

A sacristan prepares the fire for the Easter Vigil.

Prepare the tapers for the ministers and the assembly.

Reserve the seating for the elect, and, if needed, prepare the rooms where they will put on their white garments following their Baptism. Prepare the candles they will receive following Baptism. Prepare the chrism for their Confirmation.

Tonight of all nights the font should be spotlessly clean. If you have a heater, turn it on early.

Prepare a bowl and fresh branch or the aspergillum for the sprinkling of the assembly with the baptismal water.

Prepare the altar with the finest altar cloth, and place fresh candles at the altar. Be sure these will be easy to light during the Gloria at the Easter Vigil.

Review in advance the plan for turning out the electric lights. Are there emergency lights that must stay on? Is there outdoor lighting that might create a problem? Prepare your plan in advance.

EASTER SUNDAY: On Easter Sunday, notice that the Renewal of Baptismal Promises and the Rite of Sprinkling may take the place of the Creed. The texts are found among the prayers for the Easter Vigil.

Easter Time

In many parishes, the Rite of Sprinkling is used throughout Easter Time. Keep the fonts fresh and clean. Replace dying flowers—the sanctuary should always look like new life has sprung! Replant annual bulbs on the church grounds.

Ordinary Time

Ordinary Time, as all those involved in the celebration of the liturgy are aware, is anything but ordinary. The weeks of Ordinary Time—in the winter, between the feast of the Baptism of the Lord and Ash Wednesday; in the summer and fall, between Pentecost and Advent—are the largest portion of the liturgical year. Ordinary Time is all about discipleship, as the Gospel takes us through the active ministry of Jesus, healing, teaching, and redeeming. In the life of the parish, there are special moments throughout Ordinary Time—celebrations of Baptisms and other special rites, patronal feast days and dedication anniversaries, and so much more.

MOST HOLY BODY AND BLOOD OF CHRIST (*CORPUS CHRISTI*): If you observe the traditional procession with the Blessed Sacrament on this day, prepare in advance. Clean the monstrance. Prepare the cope and humeral veil. If a canopy is used, prepare it well in advance. Walk through the procession route ahead of time. If the children scatter flower petals in the outdoor procession, find out who in the parish has flourishing rose bushes and ask them to come early that morning with flowers. Fully bloomed roses work best, and they last longer if they are kept on the stem until you are ready to pull the petals off and place them in baskets for the children. Peonies and many other flowers that are easy to "depetal" work just as well as roses.

OTHER THINGS TO NOTE: In addition to these major seasons of the liturgical year, some other days require special attention from the sacristan as well. February 2 is the feast of the Presentation of the Lord, with the traditional blessing of candles. Be sure to stock up on candles for the altar, the shrines, the processional candlesticks, and the like beforehand, so that these can be blessed during the Mass. Prepare the candles for the people to carry in the procession.

February 3 is the optional memorial of Saint Blaise, with the traditional blessing of throats. While several firms offer elaborate candles for this feast, nothing fancy is needed. Just take two long, slender candles, and tie them together close to the bottom with a red ribbon. These crossed candles can then be placed on the shoulders of the person to be blessed. It will be helpful to prepare small cards with the text of the prayer of blessing for the priest and ministers to use.

November 9 is the feast of the Dedication of Saint John Lateran, one of the four major basilicas in Rome. On this day, it is appropriate to light the dedication candles in your own church, if you have them.

Working with Other Ministers

The sacristan works alone much of the time—polishing brass, cleaning and preparing vessels, tidying the sanctuary and nave. But as the "minister to the ministers," the sacristan must also be a people person. On a regular basis you will interact with many different ministers. Be as clear as possible about who directs your ministry as sacristan. Who can you go to with questions? Often, that's the liturgist or the pastor. Being clear about where your guidance comes from can simplify your life and keep the lines of communication clear.

Given the number of people involved in the liturgy, some friction is inevitable at times. The Church is made up of human beings, after all, and when human beings care passionately about something (as we all do about the liturgy) we sometimes push our point of view pretty firmly. While the sacristy can be a whirlwind of activity, especially on the big occasions of the year, the sacristan should be an oasis of peace, a calm eye in the midst of the bustle. Be flexible, and take each moment as it comes. Do not be so attached to one way of doing things that it is impossible for you to accept a change.

When tensions do arise, be the peacemaker. Find a middle way. Avoid the temptation to dissect the liturgy the moment it concludes. If mistakes occurred, those who made them are usually

When tensions do arise, be the peacemaker.

all-too-aware of the fact; wait an hour, or even a day or two, before analyzing what went wrong. If it's important, you will certainly remember the details the next day. If you forget them, then the issue was probably not as serious as it seemed at the time.

The sacristan is responsible for so many details that it can be all too easy to lose sight of the bigger picture. Find a way to participate fully in the Mass. And don't let your ministry as sacristan deprive you of the rest that comes with the Lord's Day!

Keeping Things Clean

A good sacristan keeps things neat, tidy, and organized.

No matter what your parish is like, large or small, new or old, traditional or contemporary, as sacristan you will find yourself surrounded by a huge variety of things to keep beautiful. Gold, brass, bronze, pewter, and other metals; wood, marble, slate, stone; glass, porcelain; linen, wool, silk, polyester: all of these requires different methods of cleaning. Research the best way to clean each item before you attempt to clean it. When trying out a new cleaner, always test a small, invisible area first to ensure that the results are what you hope. You don't want to discover the hard way that a beautiful image of the Blessed Virgin Mary was painted in water-soluble colors, or that an antique brass candelabra was intended to have that dark patina. A little research goes a long way. Here are some ideas for handling some of the most common cleaning tasks.

Altar Linens

Altar linens should be carefully rinsed in the sacrarium, then laundered as usual and carefully pressed. Removing lipstick or red wine stains from purificators is a constant challenge. After rinsing the cloth in the sacrarium, try sprinkling salt or club soda onto the damp stain and letting it set for two or three minutes. Rinse with cold water. Repeat as needed. You might also try a commercial stain remover or bleach stick. Your local religious supply store may also be able to recommend a stain remover especially designed to remove wine stains.

Brass and Silver

Brass and silver candlesticks, processional crosses, and other liturgical fixtures can tarnish, especially those that are regularly handled and carried in procession. There are many different metal polishes on the market, and you can experiment with these. But folk remedies—a mixture of toothpaste and Worcestershire sauce, or even ketchup—have been known to work just as well. Apply with a soft cloth, rub vigorously, rinse or remove with a dry cloth, and buff. Be cautious about using commercial metal polishes on intricately carved metal pieces, for example, on an elaborate candlestick, monstrance, or thurible. If the polish is not completely removed, it can leave an unpleasant, whitish residue in the dainty cracks and crevices. One way to avoid this is to remove the last bits of polish with a damp toothbrush. Others recommend rinsing monstrances and other gold items in white vinegar to clean them. No matter what you use, keep in mind that the "elbow grease" you use in polishing will be more effective than anything you can buy!

Candles

Keep candles clean by using followers of brass or glass, which help the candle to burn evenly, and prevent those romantic-looking but messy cascades of wax from streaming down the side of the candle. Even with followers, candles can get messy, especially in a drafty space. Remove hardened wax from the side gently with a knife. And a nylon stocking is perfect for polishing the surface of the candle, removing fingerprints and impurities without damaging the wax.

Vestments and Albs

How you clean vestments depends on the nature of the fabric. The vast majority of chasubles and dalmatics should be dry-cleaned only. Many albs, however, can be laundered in the washing machine—always check the label. In using commercial stain removers on any kind of fabric, always test in an invisible place to see how the fabric reacts.

Removing Wax

Remove wax from fabric or from carpets by laying down one or more paper towels on the spot, and running a hot iron over the towels. Replace the towels as the hot wax soaks into them. Remove wax from a smooth wood, marble, or stone surface by gently scraping it with a butter knife or spatula. You can rub a piece of ice over the wax first to make it easier to remove. You can get wax off a rough or ornamental surface by pouring boiling water over the spot. If the candleholder is small enough, you can put the whole thing in the freezer. Once it is frozen, the wax can be scraped away with ease.

Sacristy Storage

Some of the items kept in the sacristy are used every day, others are used only at particular seasons, and still others are used only one day a year. Keep this in mind in the way you arrange your sacristy. Items that are used each week should be in the most accessible places. Sort out the occasional items—like the containers to hold ashes on Ash Wednesday, the candles for the blessing of throats on the memorial of Saint Blaise, and the Advent wreath—and keep them at the back of a drawer or in that cupboard that is so high off the ground you need a stepladder to reach it. Make every effort to put things away after each liturgy. If the leftover palms are still strewn over the counter on Pentecost, or if you find yourself putting away Easter decor on the First Sunday of Advent, there's a problem! Keeping the sacristy current is just as important as keeping it clean. It is an indication to all who use the sacristy that everything used for the liturgy is cared for and treated with respect.

Historic items, including sacred vessels and vestments, require special treatment. Vessels should be kept in soft cloth bags (available from most silversmiths, and easy to make as well). Historic vestments and linens should be wrapped in acid-free paper and stored in a dry place. If you know the history of a particular piece, be sure to jot it down and keep it with the item. An inventory is a good idea (sometimes this is required for insurance purposes). It is also helpful to have a common language for referring to items that are used regularly. That way, instead of asking for "the big square red banner with the yellow flames in the middle," you can say, "the Pentecost banner."

For the sacristan, "spring cleaning" isn't always possible—with all the preparations we need to make for Lent and Easter Time, it's one of the busiest times in the liturgical year. Instead, plan to overhaul the sacristy during the quiet weeks of the summer. Reconsider the arrangement of items in the sacristy, send vestments out for dry-cleaning, and get caught up on your polishing. Sort through the purificators and linens and set aside any that are too worn or too stained to be used in the liturgy. Vestments that are no longer used can become part of an archive of historic items, or donated to a community that can use them. For more ideas on disposing of unusable items, see "Frequently Asked Questions."

Questions for Discussion and Reflection

1. What aspects of the ministry of sacristan bring you the most joy? What aspects do you find most challenging?

_____

_____

_____

2. As you prepare the church for worship, how do you prepare your heart for worship?

_____

_____

_____

3. Sacristans often find themselves doing difficult, tedious, smelly work—whether it is polishing brass, scraping gum off pews, or getting a nasty stain out of a carpet. Do you see such tasks as ministry? How?

_____

_____

_____

NOTES

1. GIRM, 105a.

2. See BB, 1853.

3. See GIRM, 304.

4. BB, 1357.

5. Ibid.

6. GIRM, 292.

7. *Built of Living Stones* (BLS), 236–237.

8. Sample formulae are provided in Appendix V.

9. See *Liturgiam authenticam*, 120.

10. *Rite of Dedication of a Church*, 71.

11. See BLS, 16.

12. See BLS, 17.

13. See BLS, 28, 31.

14. GIRM, 296.

15. BLS, 61.

16. GIRM, 310.

17. Ibid.

18. See GIRM, 314.

19. For more guidance on what worthy materials might be, consult *Built of Living Stones: Art, Architecture, and Worship,* published by the United States Conference of Catholic Bishops, 2000. While no particular style is specified for liturgical vessels, they should different from ordinary vessels, designed for everyday use. In this context, the following passage is especially helpful: "Materials used for sacred vessels such as the chalice and paten should be worthy, solid, and durable, and should not break easily. Chalices and cups used for the distribution of the Precious Blood should have bowls made of non-absorbent material. Vessels made from metal are gilded on the inside if the metal ordinarily rusts" (164). The use of local materials, whether in articles like vessels or in the building of a new church, is especially encouraged (164; 215). *Redemptionis Sacramentum* further states that "reprobated, therefore, is any practice of using for the celebration of Mass common vessels, or others lacking in quality, or devoid of all artistic merit or which are mere containers, as also other vessels made from glass, earthenware, clay, or other materials that break easily. This norm is to be applied even as regards metals and other materials that easily rust or deteriorate" (117).

20. GIRM, 314.

21. Ibid.

22. GIRM, 316.

23. The ambry may also be located in the sanctuary.

24. BLS, 117.

25. Ibid.

26. GIRM, 375.

27. Only the *Book of the Gospels* is used in liturgical processions.

28. GIRM, 85.

29. The color for funerals is usually white, although violet and black are also options.

30. Incense may be used at all the times that incense may be used at any other Mass. It may be lit before Mass begins and used at the Entrance, Gospel, and Presentation and Preparation of the Gifts and to incense each of the sacred species at the consecration.

31. This is an optional rite.

32. The rite does not specify a vessel is to be used.

33. See the *Rite of Christian Initiation of Adults* (RCIA), 481.

34. *Paschale Solemnitatis* (PS), 82.

35. Ibid.

Frequently Asked Questions

---

1. *What is the Ordo? How do I use it?*

The Ordo (Latin for *order*) is a liturgical almanac, published annually. You will need to use the Ordo that is specific to your diocese or religious community. The Ordo includes an entry for every day of the liturgical year, and includes all the information you need to prepare for the Mass. It tells you the liturgical color of the day, it explains where to find the readings and the presidential prayers, and includes notes about the Liturgy of the Hours. It also includes a variety of options—optional memorials of the saints, for example, as well as special observances like the World Day of Prayer for the Sick. Some Ordos include other useful information, like the Pope's prayer intentions for each month, and the local necrology, that is, the list of names of deceased bishops and priests of your diocese. The shorthand the Ordo uses can take some getting used to, but once you get the hang of it you will find it an invaluable resource for preparing for the liturgy.

Here's a sample day from a typical Ordo, followed by an explanation of how to read it. Usually you'll find a key to the abbreviations at the beginning of the Ordo; you might even tear that page out and use it as a bookmark through the year, until you memorize the abbreviations.

Aug 9 Saturday: Weekday [18]; *Saint Teresa Benedicta of the Cross,*		
m		*virgin; martyr; BVM on Saturday*
Gr	HOURS	**Pss II** Seasonal wkdy *Sanctoral Common*
Rd		*of one martyr or of virgins Common of BVM on Sat*
Wh		EP I of Sun: begin **Pss III**
V³R³	MASS	any Mass *or of either mem*
	RDGS	412: Hb 1:12–2:4 Ps 9:8–13 Mt 17:14–20

The top line tells us the day and date: Saturday, August 9. It tells us that this is a weekday; and the number 18 in brackets tells us that we are in the Eighteenth Week in Ordinary Time. After that, in italics, we see that there are two optional memorials on this day. (Note that italics generally mean optional. The lowercase "m" in the left hand margin indicates that today's memorials are optional. On an obligatory memorial, feast, or solemnity, you would see a capital M, F, or S.) The first is the saint of the day, Saint Teresa Benedicta of the Cross, or Edith Stein, the Carmelite martyr. The other optional memorial is the traditional remembrance of the Blessed Virgin Mary on Saturday. This means that the priest has some choices today. He can wear green and use the prayers and readings of the day (the ferial weekday). He can wear red and celebrate the memorial of Saint Teresa Benedicta of the Cross, or he can wear white and offer Mass in honor of the Blessed Virgin Mary. (Note that the colors are indicated by the abbreviations Gr, Rd, and Wh on the left-hand margin. The fact that red and white are in italics indicates that they are optional.) It is good, if possible, to find out in advance which of the memorials—if any—the priest would like to celebrate.

The next three lines give us details about the celebration of the Liturgy of the Hours. "Pss II" means that we are in Week II of the four-week Psalter, and so we can simply turn to Saturday of Week II if we wish (the ferial weekday). The italics indicate other options—today, we can pray the office from the common of one martyr or of virgins in honor of Saint Teresa, or we can pray the office from the Common of the Blessed Virgin Mary on Saturday.

The next line tells us about Evening Prayer (EP), which on this Saturday evening anticipates the coming Sunday. In the Liturgy of the Hours, two offices of Evening Prayer are prayed each Sunday of the year, called "Evening Prayer I" and "Evening Prayer II." Evening Prayer I is prayed on Saturday evening, Evening Prayer II on Sunday Evening. With Evening Prayer I on Saturday evening, we begin a new week in the four-week Psalter. This example from the Ordo tells us to turn to Week III of the Psalter.

For the "high seasons" of the liturgical year, including Advent, Christmas Time, Lent, and Easter Time, The Roman Missal provides proper prayers not only for the Sundays but for every day of the week. In Ordinary Time, however, just one set of prayers is provided for each Sunday, to be used throughout the week that follows. To vary the prayers at weekday Mass, the priest may choose from among any of the prayers given for Ordinary Time, or from the Votive Masses and Masses for Various Needs and Occasions. Prayers are also included for the First Week in Ordinary Time.

The next line takes us some of the options for the Mass. V³, in the Ordo we are using as a sample, indicates that the priest may (in place of either the liturgy of the day or the optional memorials) choose a Votive Mass, a Ritual Mass, or one of the Masses for Various Needs and Occasions. R³ means that funeral Masses as well as other Masses for the Dead are also permitted. Because this particular example from the Ordo is a day in Ordinary Time, the priest may choose "any Mass" as we see in the notations that follow. He can use any the prayers for the current week in Ordinary Time. Or he can select any of the prayers of Ordinary Time, the optional memorials of the day, or any Votive Mass, Ritual Mass, or Mass for Various Needs and Occasions. There are many options.

The final line in this entry in the Ordo gives us the readings of the day. The number "412" is the Lectionary number, and the full citations are included as well.

2. What is The Roman Missal? Is that different from The Sacramentary?

In the early centuries of the Church, several different books were used for the celebration of the Mass—a "Sacramentary" which contained the priest's prayers, a "Lectionary" that contained the readings, and an "Evangeliary," or *Book of the Gospels*. Later on, books began to be prepared that combined both readings and prayers in one. This kind of book was known as a *Missale Plenum*, that is, "complete missal" (the Latin word *missalis* means having to do with the Mass). From the time of the Council of Trent, there was just one book containing both the readings and prayers of the Mass, called the *Missale Romanum*.

Following the Second Vatican Council, the readings used in the liturgy were vastly expanded, and it became impractical to put all the texts for the Mass in one volume. The tradition of separate "Sacramentaries" and "Lectionaries" was restored. However, the term *Missale Romanum* continued to be used to describe the Latin edition of what we came to know as *The Sacramentary*. The new English translation of the third typical edition of the *Missale Romanum* accurately translates the title of the volume: *The Roman Missal*. Though the terms can be confusing, *The Roman Missal* and *The Sacramentary* refer to the same book containing the prayers of the Mass of the Roman Rite. However, the book is no longer being referred to as *The Sacramentary*, and from now on, will be called *The Roman Missal*.

3. What does it mean to "purify" the sacred vessels? Is that different from cleaning the vessels after Mass?

The vessels used to contain the consecrated bread and wine during the Mass receive a special cleansing called "purification" following Holy Communion or immediately following Mass. This purification stems from our Catholic belief in the real presence of Christ in Eucharist, and is carried out to ensure that any particles of the sacred species that may have remained in the paten or the chalice are reverently consumed. This rite of purification is carried out by a priest, deacon, or instituted acolyte.

Following Holy Communion or Mass, usually at the credence table, the paten and ciboria are carefully wiped over a chalice, so that any crumbs or fragments that remain can be collected. Any remaining Precious Blood is consumed, and then the chalices are rinsed with water (or with a mixture of wine and water, according to local custom), which the minister then consumes.

After this rite of purification, the vessels are ready to be cleaned by the sacristan or another minister: they are carefully rinsed in the sacrarium, and then washed and dried in the usual way.[1]

4. Are there special requirements for cleaning sacred things—linens and vestments, the sacrarium, or holy water fonts? What about disposing of blessed items that we can no longer use?

Vestments worn by the priest, deacon, and other ministers should be cared for as you would any fine garments—pressed and cleaned regularly, dry-cleaned if necessary. Careful storage of vestments will help to avoid extra trips to the dry-cleaners, which is expensive and can also shorten the life of the vestment.

Linens that have been used during Mass or Communion services, however—including altar cloths, corporals, and purificators—require special attention. Altar cloths and corporals can generally be used several times, but they should be checked carefully after each Mass to ensure that no crumbs are left (this is part of the purification of the vessels; see above). Before being laundered, they should be carefully rinsed in the sacrarium. Purificators need to be washed after every use. They are rinsed carefully in the sacrarium before being laundered in the usual way.

When cleaning the holy water fonts, the holy water left in the font should be collected and poured into the sacrarium; the fonts may then be cleaned in any appropriate way. If the fonts are fixed to the wall, this can be challenging. You might take a bucket, and gather the water in a smaller vessel or cup, then dry whatever remains at the bottom with a clean towel (the towel could then be rinsed in the sacrarium when you empty the water into it).

The same goes for blessed ashes left over after Ash Wednesday: the ashes can be rinsed down the sacrarium or buried, and the vessels should be rinsed in the sacrarium before being washed in the usual way.

Take special care in disposing of blessed articles. For large items—vestments, statues, books, hymnal sets, and the like—it is possible that another parish in your diocese, or a sister parish in another country, could use the articles you no longer need. Often your diocesan Office of Divine Worship will be able to help you to offer such items to another parish community. They will also be able to let you know about guidelines for disposing of such articles as worn-out purificators and the like in your diocese. In some places, it is customary to burn articles like blessed purificators, altar cloths, or vestments that are no longer usable. But consider the possibilities before doing so. An altar cloth might be cut down into several corporals or many purificators. And a vestment that cannot be used in the liturgy might be cleverly transformed into a vestment for the Infant of Prague, if you have such an image in your church. Unusable fabric could be cut into small pieces and used to start the Easter fire. There are many possibilities.

> ✠ "Reverence for sacred things continues even after they are no longer useful in the liturgy."
> —BLS, 237

5. How can I make our sacristy more eco-friendly?

Keeping the sacristy clean in responsible ways is more than a nice option—it's a responsibility! Take the initiative to look into ways to make sure your sacristy is a model of good stewardship of the earth.[2] Here are some ideas.

- Use old paperwork, whether extra copies of intercessions or bulletin inserts, as scratch paper. Rinse wine bottles and take them away for recycling. If you use disposable worship aids, be sure they get recycled when they are no longer usable; however, consider using permanent hymnals instead of disposable worship aids or missals.

- In many areas, compost pickup is available. Scraps of food and even things like leftover napkins can be tossed in the compost bin, and so can faded flower arrangements, potted plants, and many of the other living decorations used in the church. All of these things would otherwise go into a landfill, so compost service is well worth the investment if it is available in your area.

- Look into safe methods of disposing of batteries before you throw them in the trash. You might even use rechargeable batteries.

- Consider eco-friendly cleaning supplies, more and more of which are available at a reasonable cost.

- Turn out the lights! Get in the habit of turning out the sacristy lights when you leave the room. If the church is open all day, develop a "low-light" setting for private prayer instead of turning on everything, as at Sunday Mass. If feasible in your church building, consider energy-saving bulbs.

6. *What kind of hosts and wine can be used in the liturgy?*

Hosts "must be made only from wheat, must be recently made, and, according to the ancient tradition of the Latin Church, must be unleavened."[3] The wine "must be from the fruit of the vine (cf. Lk 22:18), natural, and unadulterated, that is, without admixture of extraneous substances."[4] The bread and wine should also be fresh.[5] That means that leavened bread and fruit flavored wines may not be used for the Eucharist; nor is stale bread or wine that has turned to vinegar suitable for use in the Eucharist.

The wine used should be of good quality, but there is no requirement that it be red, nor is there any specific indication as to its alcohol content. But it must be wine, not fruit juice. Priests and members of the assembly who are unable to drink alcohol can get permission from the Bishop to use mustum (grape juice without additives of any kind), for themselves only.[6]

Another question that has come up recently is the idea of gluten-free hosts for people who are gluten intolerant. Because the hosts must be made of wheat, it is impossible to make an entirely gluten-free host. The Congregation of Benedictine Sisters of Perpetual Adoration in Clyde, Missouri, however, prepare very low-gluten hosts which have been deemed safe for those who suffer from gluten intolerance (see http://benedictinesisters.org/). Those who cannot receive even the small amount of gluten in such hosts can still receive Communion under the form of the Precious Blood. To read more about Celiac Sprue disease, visit the United States Conference of Catholic Bishops' Web site at www.usccb.org/liturgy/celiasprue.shtml.

NOTES

1. See GIRM, 278–280.

2. Go to http://earth911.org/ for helpful advise regarding ways to go green.

3. GIRM, 320. See especially GIRM, 319–322.

4. GIRM, 322.

5. See GIRM, 323.

6. See Prot. 89/78-174, 98.

Resources

Church Documents

Built of Living Stones: Art, Architecture, and Worship (2000). This document from the United States Conference of Catholic Bishops is intended primarily as a guide to building or renovating churches, but it is useful for all who are involved in the liturgy or in the maintenance of a church building.

Constitution on the Sacred Liturgy (1963). This first of the four constitutions of the Second Vatican Council laid the groundwork for the reform of the liturgy. It is still the most important Church document on liturgy. Available in LTP's *The Liturgy Documents: A Parish Resource*, Volume I.

General Instruction of the Roman Missal (revised edition, 2010). This document is often published separately but really forms the introduction to *The Roman Missal*. It provides detailed instructions about the celebration of the liturgy, about the ministry of the deacon, about concelebration, and provides along the way much wisdom about the nature of the liturgy.

Paschale Solemnitatis: A Circular Letter Concerning Preparing and Celebrating the Easter Feasts. A document released by the Congregation for Divine Worship and the Discipline of the Sacraments in 1988. It is full of invaluable guidance on preparing for the Triduum in union with the whole Church. It is found in LTP's *The Liturgy Documents: A Parish Resource*, volume II.

Pastoral Resources

At the Supper of the Lamb: A Pastoral and Theological Commentary on the Mass. Turner, Paul. This book walks you through each part of the Mass. Its structure follows the Order of Mass in the third edition of *The Roman Missal* and is an invitation to worship, a call to new intention, and a deeper awareness of the privilege we share to be invited to the supper of the Lamb.

The Church at Prayer. Martimort, A. G. You might want to dip into A. G. Martimort's *The Church at Prayer,* a four-volume exploration of the history of the liturgy, the liturgical year, and the rites of the Church.

Pastoral Liturgy.™ This 32-page, full-color magazine follows the course of the liturgical year to provide guidance for liturgy preparation, faith formation, liturgical art and architecture, and the many areas of parish ministry that flow from the liturgy to witness the Gospel and build the kingdom of God. *Pastoral Liturgy*™ is the liturgy magazine for the whole parish!

The Sacristy Manual. Ryan, G. Thomas. LTP, 1993. This is *the* book for sacristans, including detailed information on everything from storing vestments to preparing for a visiting Bishop. It is an invaluable resource, especially the detailed checklists for the rites and for the principal celebrations of the liturgical year. At the time of this printing, a second edition is being prepared.

Sourcebook for Sundays, Seasons, and Weekdays: The Almanac for Pastoral Liturgy. This annual publication from LTP provides commentary on the readings of the year, as well as plenty of background information on the feasts and suggestions on how to prepare for them. It is an excellent resource to use in conjunction with your local Ordo.

Glossary

ALB: A long, white garment, worn by priests, deacons, and by lay ministers as well. It is a reminder of the white garment given in Baptism.

AMBRY: The place where the oil of catechumens, the oil of the sick, and the sacred chrism are kept.

AMICE: A square, white cloth which is tied around the neck to cover the collar; used when the alb does not cover the collar completely.

ASPERGILLUM: An instrument used for the sprinkling of holy water; a live branch can also be used as an aspergillum.

BAPTISTRY: The place in the church building where the font for Baptism is located.

BOBECHE: A disk or "collar" of metal, glass, plastic, or paper used to catch the wax dripping down a candle.

CASSOCK: A long garment, usually black, which buttons or snaps down the front, worn with a surplice.

CHALICE: A cup used to hold the Precious Blood during Mass.

CHASUBLE: The priestly vestment worn only for the celebration of Mass.

CIBORIUM: A covered vessel used to hold consecrated hosts/bread.

CINCTURE: A belt, usually white, which is sometimes used with an alb.

COMMON: Refers to prayers that can be used for a variety of different commemorations—*The Roman Missal* includes Common of Dedication of a Church, Common of the Blessed Virgin Mary, and Commons for many different categories of saints.

COPE: A cape-like vestment worn by a priest or deacon for liturgies outside Mass, like the Liturgy of the Hours; also worn for processions on Palm Sunday and the Most Holy Body and Blood of Christ (*Corpus Christi*).

CORPORAL: A square, white cloth placed over the altar cloth on which the chalice and paten are placed at the Presentation and Preparation of the Gifts.

CREDENCE TABLE: A table, usually located in the sanctuary, where the vessels and other necessary items are placed for the celebration of Mass.

CROSIER: A staff carried by the Bishop of a diocese in procession; it usually resembles a shepherd's staff.

DALMATIC: A vestment that may be worn by the deacon for the celebration of Mass.

FONT: A vessel containing holy water used for the celebration of the sacrament of Baptism.

FRONTAL: A cloth that hangs down the front of an altar, often in the liturgical color, also known as an antependium.

GREMIALE: A cloth spread over the lap of the Bishop to protect his vestments during anointing.

HUMERAL VEIL: A cloth placed around the shoulders of a priest or deacon when he carries the Blessed Sacrament, whether in procession or for benediction of the Blessed Sacrament.

LAVABO: A pitcher and basin used for the washing of the priest's hands during Mass.

LECTIONARY FOR MASS: One of the indispensable liturgical books of the Mass, it contains the readings for Sundays and weekdays for the entire liturgical year.

LITURGY OF THE HOURS: Called "the prayer of the Church,"[1] the primary offices of the Liturgy of the Hours are Morning Prayer and Evening Prayer. It consists largely of the chanting or recitation of Psalms. The Liturgy of the Hours is prayed daily by bishops, priests, and religious throughout the world.

LUCERNARIUM: A ceremonial lighting of candles, which sometimes takes place as part of the Evening Prayer in the Liturgy of the Hours.

MITER: The pointed hat worn by a Bishop during celebrations of the liturgy.

MONSTRANCE: A transparent vessel in which a consecrated host is to be placed so as to be seen by the faithful.

NAVE: The main body of a church, so called from its imagined resemblance to a ship.

OFFERTORY TABLE: A small table, usually located in the nave, where the gifts of bread and wine are placed to be brought forward in procession by members of the assembly.

ORDINARY: In *The Roman Missal,* "ordinary" refers to those parts of the liturgy that are repeated at every Mass—it includes the formulas for the Penitential Act, the Gloria, the Creed, the prayers for the Preparation of the Gifts, and the Eucharistic Prayers.

ORDO: A book or leaflet, published locally or regionally, giving detailed information about each day of the liturgical year.

OSTENSORIUM: Another name for a monstrance (see above).

PALL: At funerals, a large cloth, usually white, which is placed over the coffin as a reminder of Baptism. Pall is also the name for a square of fabric sometimes used to cover the chalice and paten on the credence table before the liturgy.

PATEN: A small plate used by the priest to hold the hosts. Ciboria (see above) are generally used for distribution of Holy Communion.

PREFACE: The Preface is the first part of the Eucharistic Prayer. It is spoken or sung by the priest and concludes with the entire assembly's singing of the Holy, Holy, Holy.

PROPER: Refers to a part of the Mass which is unique ("proper") to a particular season or saint. Two major portions of the prayers of *The Roman Missal* include the "Proper of Time" and the "Proper of Saints."

PURIFICATOR: A small cloth, usually white, used to wipe the rim of the cup during the Communion Rite at Mass.

PYX: A small container, usually of metal, used for holding consecrated hosts.

THE ROMAN MISSAL: One of the most important liturgical books used during Mass, it contains all the prayers the priest will need during Mass.

ROMAN PONTIFICAL: Ritual book containing rites at which a Bishop usually presides, such as Confirmation, ordinations, and the dedication of a church, among others.

SACRARIUM: A special sink installed in a sacristy for the cleaning of sacred vessels. It drains directly into the earth, not into the sewer.

SANCTUARY: That area of the church building that contains the altar, ambo, and presidential chair.

SANCTUARY LAMP: A candle or oil lamp that both indicates and gives honor to the presence of the Blessed Sacrament in the tabernacle of a church building.

STOLE: A narrow strip of fabric worn by ordained ministers with liturgical vestments. Priests wear the stole around the neck, hanging down in front. Deacons wear it over the left shoulder, across the chest, and pinned at the right side.

SURPLICE: A short white garment worn over a cassock.

TABERNACLE: A large, permanent container for the consecrated hosts reserved in a church building.

THURIBLE: A vessel for carrying incense in procession. It is usually made of metal and hangs from a chain. The thurifer is the minister who carries the thurible or censer in procession.

VESTMENTS: The special garments worn by the ministers of the liturgy.

VIMPA: A cloth placed around the shoulders of a server. It is used to hold the miter and crosier when the Bishop is present.

VOTIVE MASS: A Mass said during Ordinary Time in honor of a mystery of the Lord (for example, the Holy Cross, the Precious Blood, the Eucharist), the Blessed Virgin Mary, the angels, or one of the saints.

ZUCCHETTO: A skullcap worn by bishops and others: white for the pope, red for cardinals, purple for bishops and archbishops, and black for abbots.

NOTES

1 *General Instruction of the Liturgy of the Hours*, 1.

I'm setting out the vessels, Lord.
I'm reaching for cups and plates, pitchers, and bowls.
Now they are empty.
Soon they will hold the bread and wine that
     will become your body and blood.
Make me a vessel, Lord.
Open my heart and make me you to all I meet today.
Amen.

I'm cleaning up, Lord.
I'm tired, but I'm scrubbing.
Clean me, Lord, would you?
Do not tire of me when I am stained with sin.
Purify me.
Amen.